California
Travel Guide
2023

The Complete Travel Guide To Explore
The Beauty Of California

Kay F. Raap

TABLE OF CONTENTS

INTRODUCTION

Welcome to California, a vibrant and diverse state where dreams come true and stunning scenery draws tourists from all over the world. Your key to discovering the treasures and pleasures that await you in this golden land of limitless opportunities is this thorough California Travel Guide Book 2023.

With its sandy beaches, majestic mountains, thriving towns, and enthralling natural wonders, California offers a tapestry of experiences that may satisfy any traveler's needs. California has it all, whether you're looking for the glitz of Hollywood, the peace of old redwood forests, the thrill of surfing on gorgeous beaches, or the gourmet delights of renowned vineyards.

We've painstakingly gathered a plethora of knowledge and insider advice in this carefully curated guidebook to make sure your trip across California is nothing short of exceptional. We'll take you on an exciting journey as we reveal the must-see sights, secret treasures, and unusual locations that capture the spirit of this gorgeous state.

Visit the famed wineries of Napa Valley or see the magnificent Golden Gate Bridge as it towers majestically against the backdrop of San Francisco's skyline. Get lost in Yosemite National Park's magnificent surroundings, where colossal granite cliffs and tumbling waterfalls form a mesmerizing symphony of nature. Discover the lively spirit of Los Angeles, the center of the entertainment industry, where imagination and ambitions converge.

However, California is much more than its well-known monuments. Off the usual road, you can find hidden gems that are waiting to be discovered. Explore Big Sur's magnificent coastline scenery, relax in the quaint communities of Monterey and Carmel, or find peace among the historic giants of the Redwood National and State Parks. Immerse yourself in Santa Barbara's diverse cultural heritage or Santa Cruz's laid-back surf scene.

This guidebook goes beyond simple sightseeing by giving you useful details on available modes of transportation, suggested lodgings, food alternatives, and priceless travel advice to make your trip effortless and unforgettable. We also provide information on the state's many climates so you can confidently plan your trip and make the most of your time in each area.

Let this book be your dependable travel companion as you set off on this voyage through California, illuminating the way to amazing encounters and priceless memories. Allow yourself to be enthralled by the attraction of this extraordinary state, where dreams come true and unforgettable experiences lie around every corner, whether you're a first-time visitor or an experienced tourist.

Flip through the pages, take in the vivid hues, engrossing tales, and helpful advice inside, then get ready to set out on a tour that will leave you permanently entranced by California's charm.

Welcome to your entryway to the Golden State, the California Travel Guide Book 2023. The journey has begun!

HISTORY OF CALIFORNIA

The threads of indigenous cultures, Spanish colonization, Mexican rule, and the final conversion into an American state are woven together throughout the history of California to make a tapestry. California's history spans the earliest days of human existence to the present and is characterized by diversity, ingenuity, and perpetual change.

The Native American tribes were the first people to live in the area that is now California. Before European explorers arrived, these indigenous peoples—among them the Miwok, Pomo, Chumash, and several others—succumbed in the rich natural resources of the area.

The first European to set foot on Californian soil was the Portuguese explorer Juan Rodrguez Cabrillo in 1542. However, Spanish colonization did not start in earnest until the late 18th century. To bolster Spain's position in the region, Gaspar de Portolá led an expedition in 1769 that founded a string of missions and presidios, including the renowned Mission San Diego de Alcalá.

Spanish soldiers and missionaries grew their influence during the following few decades, establishing a network of 21 missions along the California coast. These missions sought to evangelize and assimilate Native Americans into Spanish colonial civilization. They had a big influence on the state's architectural and cultural legacy.

When Mexico won its independence from Spain in 1821, California was included in Mexican territory. Significant changes were brought about under Mexican control, such as the secularization of the missions and the creation of sizable ranchos owned by Mexican settlers. The ranchos developed as the hub of agricultural output, with farming and cattle grazing influencing the environment.

California's history underwent major changes throughout the 19th century. California was given to the United States as part of the Treaty of Guadalupe Hidalgo, which was signed in 1848 and put an end to the Mexican-American War. The California Gold Rush started the next year after gold was found at Sutter's Mill in Coloma.

California had a quick population explosion due to the influx of thousands of people looking for their fortune from around the world, which also drastically changed the area's economy and society.

California was admitted to as the 31st state in 1850 to the union. Cities like San Francisco and Sacramento, as well as expanding sectors like mining, transportation, and agriculture, were all significantly impacted by the Gold Rush. California was further connected to the rest of the nation with the Transcontinental Railroad's completion in 1869, which helped the state's economy grow.

The late 19th and early 20th centuries saw considerable expansion and diversification in California. With breakthroughs in agriculture, technology, aircraft, and entertainment, the state developed into a hub of innovation and business. Hollywood's film industry rose to prominence and came to represent the glitz and innovation of California.

Additionally, California has been a major player in a number of social and cultural movements. It has been a hub for activity, including the labor movement, the civil rights movement, the environmental movement, and the advocacy for LGBTQ+ rights. With the rise of the hippie movement in San Francisco's Haight-Ashbury neighborhood, the counterculture of the 1960s found a thriving home in California.

California continues to be one of the most populated and prosperous states in the country today. People from all walks of life continue to be drawn to it by its diversified population, breathtaking natural surroundings, and energetic cities. California's history and current vibrancy continue to influence its future as a beacon of opportunity and hope, from the towering redwood forests to the sun-drenched beaches, from Silicon Valley's technological advances to the agricultural heartland of the Central Valley.

CHAPTER 1

WELCOME TO CALIFORNIA

CALIFORNIA AT A GLANCE

California is a state of amazing beauty and enormous diversity that is situated on the western coast of the United States. It is the most populated state in the nation with a total area of about 163,000 square miles (423,970 square kilometers) and over 39 million residents.

Geographically speaking, California is as diverse as its people. With scenic beaches, craggy cliffs, and famous monuments like the Golden Gate Bridge in San Francisco and the Santa Monica Pier in Los Angeles, the state has a breathtaking coastline that spans along the Pacific Ocean for over 840 miles (1,350 kilometers).

California is endowed with magnificent natural beauties inland. Magnificent mountain ranges like the Sierra Nevada and the Cascade Range with towering peaks like Mount Whitney, the highest point in the contiguous United States, tower over the landscape. The state's varied landscape is further enhanced by picturesque valleys, lush agriculture, and vast deserts, such the Mojave Desert.

The climate in California is also very diverse. Mild Mediterranean climates with mild, wet winters and pleasant, dry summers are prevalent along the coast. The climate is more continental in inland areas, with warm summers and chilly winters. A wide variety of ecosystems, from dense forests to arid desert habitats, are supported by the state's different microclimates.

The state's cultural diversity is woven into a colorful tapestry from a wide range of nationalities, languages, and customs. Immigrants from all over the world have long sought refuge in California, fostering the state's diversified civilization. It is home to the biggest concentration of Asian Americans in the country as well as sizeable Hispanic and Latino American groups.

The economy of California is the biggest in the US and among the biggest in the entire world. A wide mix of businesses, including entertainment, technology, agriculture, aerospace, tourism, and finance, are responsible for the state's economic strength. The San Francisco Bay Area's Silicon Valley is regarded as a global center for innovation and the origin of several digital juggernauts.

Additionally, the nation's top universities, such as the University of California system and the California State University system, which draw students from all over the world, are located in the state.

Beyond its importance to the economy and culture, California provides a wide range of recreational possibilities. Yosemite, Joshua Tree, and Redwood National and State Parks, which showcase breathtaking natural landscapes and a variety of animals, are just a few of the several national parks that outdoor enthusiasts can visit.

The state offers a wide variety of outdoor activities for every season, from skiing in Lake Tahoe to surfing in Santa Cruz.

Cities in California are vibrant metropolises bursting with life and diversity. The world's entertainment center, Los Angeles, enchants visitors with its legendary sites, thriving cultural community, and glitzy Hollywood charm.

The famed Golden Gate Bridge, San Francisco's steep hills, and its vintage cable cars all fascinate tourists. Other cities have their own distinctive charms and attractions, like San Diego, Sacramento, and San Jose.

California at a Glance offers a snapshot of this exceptional state's fascinating landscapes, varied cultures, growing economy, and limitless prospects, capturing the essence of this extraordinary state.

California continues to captivate hearts and minds with its sun-drenched beaches, snow-capped mountains, cultural melting pots, and technological foresight, making it a unique destination that leaves an imprint on everyone who experiences its beauty.

CLIMATE AND WEATHER

California has a wide variety of climates and weather patterns due to its enormous size and varied geography. California is home to a wide range of climatic conditions, which add to its distinctive attractiveness. These circumstances range from coastal regions to inland valleys, towering mountains to dry deserts.

California's coast is fortunate to have a Mediterranean climate. These areas experience agreeable temperatures all year round and are characterized by moderate, wet winters and warm, dry summers.

Average winter and summer temperatures in major cities like San Francisco, Los Angeles, and San Diego range from the low 50s to the mid 70s Fahrenheit (10 to 24 degrees Celsius), and from the mid-60s to the mid 80s Fahrenheit (18 to 29 degrees Celsius). Cool ocean currents have an impact on the coastal climate, and morning fog is a common occurrence, especially in the summer.

The climate changes to a more continental style as you get inland. Summers in the Central Valley are hot and dry, with temperatures frequently topping 90 degrees Fahrenheit (32 degrees Celsius). The Central Valley runs from the Sacramento region in the north to the San Joaquin Valley in the south.

Temperatures in the wintertime range from the 40s to the 60s Fahrenheit (4-16 degrees Celsius), making them colder. The Central Valley is frequently referred to as the "breadbasket of the world" due to its famed agricultural productivity.

The climate grows more alpine as you travel further inland and ascend to higher altitudes, like the Sierra Nevada mountains. Winters are bitterly cold and snowy, with lows below zero and large accumulations of snow in higher elevations. Winter sports fans have good chances in the Alps, where top-notch ski resorts draw tourists from near and far.

The cool and pleasant summers found in the highlands provide a nice respite from the oppressive heat of the lowlands.

The Mojave Desert, which is located in the southeast of the state and is distinguished by its dry climate. Summers in the desert are scorching, with frequent highs of 100 degrees Fahrenheit (38 degrees Celsius). With temperatures in the 40s to 60s Fahrenheit (4-16 degrees Celsius), winters are milder. Visitors are fascinated by the unearthly aura that the desert landscape's distinctive Joshua trees and extensive stretches of sand dunes provide.

California can experience a wide range of weather events. Periodic droughts affect the state, especially in the southern areas, and can have a serious negative impact on agricultural and water supplies. Wildfires are a constant worry, particularly in windy and dry circumstances. Fire danger may be increased by the Santa Ana winds, which are warm, dry winds coming from the inland.

Marine layer fog frequently drifts in from the ocean and is especially common in coastal locations during the summer. This fog has the potential to engulf coastal communities, impairing visibility and producing a chilly, damp atmosphere.

Visitors should keep up-to-date on the weather and be ready for any potential differences across the state's many areas. It is advised to check local forecasts and pay attention to any weather advisories or warnings, especially if you plan to travel across California or engage in outdoor activities.

Whatever your preference, California's unique temperature and weather patterns have something to offer you, whether you prefer the sea breeze, the warmth of the inland valleys, or the snow-capped peaks of the mountains. California is an interesting and dynamic destination all year round because of its diverse climates and distinctive weather experiences, which range from sunny beaches to snowy hills, from desert sunsets to foggy coastlines.

GETTING AROUND

California offers a wide range of transportation alternatives for visitors to explore its various areas because of its vastness and unique landscape. Here are several essential methods for getting around in California, whether you're navigating the busy streets of towns, traveling along picturesque coastal highways, or navigating hilly terrain.

Renting a car: is a common option for seeing California because it offers ease and flexibility. Numerous car rental companies with a variety of vehicles are present at major airports and cities. Make sure your driver's license is up to date, and learn the rules and restrictions for driving in California.

Public Transportation: The state of California is home to a vast network of buses, trains, and light rail systems. Popular tourist destinations, communities, and suburbs can all be reached by public transportation in major cities like San Francisco, Los Angeles, and San Diego. Some significant examples include the San Francisco Bay Area Rapid Transit (BART), the Los Angeles Metro, and the San Diego Metropolitan Transit System.

Ride-Sharing Services: In California's cities, ride-sharing services like Uber and Lyft are readily accessible and provide dependable and convenient transportation. Simply download the corresponding app to your smartphone, make your ride request, and a driver will come and pick you up and transport you where you need to go. When you don't want to drive or need to go small distances, this alternative is really helpful.

Intercity Buses: Intercity bus services connect various California regions and offer a cost-effective mode of transportation. It is simple to travel between cities and towns because to the routes that organizations like Greyhound, Megabus, and BoltBus operate throughout the state.

Train: Amtrak has rail services that connect California's major cities and communities. The Pacific Surfliner route follows the shore and offers breathtaking ocean vistas. The California Zephyr connects California with neighboring states, while the Capitol Corridor and San Joaquin lines provide service to interior regions.

Domestic flights: can save you time if you're going to travel over vast distances inside California. Los Angeles International Airport (LAX), San Francisco International Airport (SFO), and San Diego International Airport (SAN) are three of the state's largest airports, and they all offer a wide range of domestic flights to different locations inside the state.

Cycling: California is a great place for cycling aficionados because of its pleasant climate and beautiful scenery. It is simple to explore urban areas on two wheels because many cities have bike-sharing programs and designated bike lanes. The Pacific Coast Highway is just one of the many breathtaking cycling routes that offer a spectacular way to enjoy California's natural splendor.

Walking: Getting out and about on foot is a fantastic way to experience California's cities and communities. There are sidewalks, crosswalks, and other pedestrian-friendly infrastructure in many places, particularly in urban centers. You can experience the active street life, appreciate the distinctive charm of each district, and find hidden treasures by walking.

It's crucial to keep in mind that travel times and the accessibility of transportation may change based on your location and the time of day. Checking schedules, planning your routes beforehand, and taking into account probable traffic congestion are all recommended, especially in large cities.

Regardless of the method of transportation you use, safety should always come first. Pay attention to the state of the roads, follow posted speed limits, and be aware of any parking restrictions in cities.

Visitors may easily tour California's different areas because to the state's abundant transportation alternatives, which accommodate a wide range of tastes. Getting around in California gives the chance to embark on exciting trips and discover the many beauties this magnificent state has to offer, whether you like the freedom of a rental car, the ease of public transportation, or the excitement of cycling.

CHAPTER 2

EXPLORING-NORTHERN CALIFORNIA

SAN FRANCISCO

San Francisco is a bustling and recognizable city noted for its breathtaking natural beauty, rich cultural heritage, and forward-thinking attitude. It is located at the northernmost point of the picturesque California coast. San Francisco draws tourists from all over the world with its mountainous landscape, charming neighborhoods, and well-known attractions.

Golden Gate Bridge

The Golden Gate Bridge, which spans the entrance to San Francisco Bay, is one of the city's most identifiable emblems. Its vivid orange-red hue looks stunning against the undulating hills of Marin County and the Pacific Ocean in the distance. Cross the bridge on foot or by bicycle, or take in the spectacular scenery from one of the many vantage spots.

Fisherman's Wharf

Is a bustling, historic district on the city's northern shore that is home to a lot of activity. It has a plethora of dining establishments, gift stores, and entertainment choices. Take advantage of the opportunity to experience the renowned clam chowder served in sourdough bread bowls or go on a boat cruise to Alcatraz Island.

Alcatraz Island

Located in the center of San Francisco Bay, this island is the site of the famed old federal prison where some of the country's most notorious criminals were previously detained. Today, it is a well-liked tourist spot where guests can board a ferry to tour the prison's cells, discover its fascinating past, and take in the breathtaking views of the city skyline.

Cable Cars

San Francisco's well-known cable cars serve both a source of transit and a wonderful representation of the city. Climb aboard these antique vehicles, which are propelled by a network of underground cables, and travel the city's winding streets while taking in the surrounding scenery. Particularly well-liked lines that take visitors through the city's neighborhoods are Powell-Hyde and Powell-Mason.

Chinatown

The largest Chinatown outside of Asia, San Francisco's thriving Chinatown is a busy neighborhood full with historical and cultural gems. Discover the city's crowded streets, elaborate temples, and traditional shops selling anything from rare herbs to elaborate Chinese art. Don't forget to savor genuine cuisine at one of the area's numerous well-known eateries.

Golden Gate Park

Over 1,000 acres in size, Golden Gate Park is a lush haven in the middle of the metropolis. The de Young Museum, the California Academy of Sciences, the Japanese Tea Garden, and tranquil lakes and gardens are just a few of the many attractions it has to offer. Picnicking, jogging, cycling, and discovering the park's varied flora and wildlife are popular activities among locals and tourists alike.

Haight-Ashbury

The Haight-Ashbury district has a bohemian flair and is well-known for its ties to the counterculture and the 1960s hippie movement. It is teeming with street art, record shops, vibrant Victorian homes, and vintage businesses. Discover the bustling music and arts scene in this diverse neighborhood as you explore it and take in its distinctive atmosphere.

Embarcadero and Ferry Building

Offering breathtaking views of the San Francisco Bay, the Bay Bridge, and the city skyline, the Embarcadero is a charming waterfront promenade. Enjoy fresh seafood at the renowned restaurants that line the waterfront as you stroll along the picturesque pathway, discover the Ferry Building Marketplace with its gourmet food vendors, and explore the marketplace.

San Francisco is a city that never fails to enthrall visitors with its diverse cultural heritage, breathtaking natural surroundings, and well-known attractions. San Francisco guarantees an amazing experience that captures the distinctive character of this remarkable city, whether you're crossing the Golden Gate Bridge, immersing yourself in the history of Alcatraz, or simply taking in the colorful ambiance of its neighborhoods.

GOLDEN GATE BRIDGE

The Golden Gate Bridge, one of the most recognizable structures in the world and an iconic representation of San Francisco, rises majestically above the San Francisco Bay's glistening seas. This engineering marvel, which spans the bay's entrance, is not only a work of art in architecture but also a symbol of human ingenuity and a source of inspiration for future generations.

Iconic Beauty

The Golden Gate Bridge's vivid orange-red color contrasts tastefully with the bay's deep blue seas to create an unforgettable scene that stays in the mind of everyone who sees it. It stands as a timeless representation of San Francisco's attraction and attractiveness thanks to its imposing suspension towers and elegant Art Deco style.

Engineering Feat

The Golden Gate Bridge, which took four years to build and was finished in 1937, was a significant engineering feat for its day. One of the world's longest suspension bridges, its main span spans an astonishing 4,200 feet (1,280 meters). The bridge's cutting-edge construction makes it resistant to the region's strong winds, ocean currents, and periodic earthquakes.

Gateway to San Francisco

The Golden Gate Bridge acts as a point of entry into the thriving city of San Francisco. The bridge extends a warm welcome to all travelers, whether they are traveling by air, sea, or land. It creates a sense of arrival and expectation. The cityscape gradually appears before your eyes as you cross the bridge, showing the magnificent skyline, the glittering water, and the undulating hills that characterize this special metropolis.

Scenic Vistas

The bridge offers unmatched panoramic vistas in addition to serving as a method of transportation. Visitors are treated to expansive views of the San Francisco Bay, Alcatraz Island, the metropolitan skyline, and the rough coastline beyond from numerous vantage points along the bridge and the nearby hills.

Photographers and nature lovers alike are enthralled by the bridge's constantly shifting backdrop, whether it is shrouded in mist or glistening in the sun.

Walkable Experience

Using the authorized walkways, pedestrians and cyclists may travel the Golden Gate Bridge's 1.7-mile (2.7-kilometer) length up close and personal. You may experience the steady vibration of traffic as you cross and take in the breathtaking sights that appear with each step. Both the San Francisco and Marin County sides of the bridge have pedestrian walkways, providing a unique opportunity to explore this engineering marvel.

Engineering Landmarks

The recognizable Art Deco-style towers at each end of the bridge stand tall, directing ships and emphasizing the bridge's majesty. Visitors can visit the Bridge Pavilion, which is in the southeast corner and has displays detailing the history of the bridge, its building, and the people who made it possible. Learn about the difficulties encountered during construction and the amazing engineering achievements made to realize this goal.

The Golden Gate Bridge Never Fails to Captivate: Whether seen in the foggy morning mist, gleaming in the golden light of sunset, or illuminated against the night sky. It is a photographer's paradise and a source of inspiration for writers, artists, and dreamers from all over the world thanks to its eternal appeal and ever-changing beauty.

More than just a way to cross the bay, the Golden Gate Bridge is a revered symbol of San Francisco's character that represents the best of human ingenuity and tenacity. This recognizable bridge creates an indelible impression on everyone who has the opportunity to experience its beauty, whether that impression comes from admiring its architectural magnificence, becoming lost in its history, or simply taking in its breathtaking vistas.

FISHERMAN'S WHARF

Fisherman's Wharf is a bustling and historic district that is tucked away along San Francisco's scenic waterfront. It is full of alluring views, mouthwatering cuisine, and a lively environment. This famous location, which is rich in maritime history, gives tourists a taste of San Francisco's fascinating past and a wide range of enjoyable experiences.

Historical Fishing Traditions

Fisherman's Wharf has a long and storied fishing tradition that dates to the founding of San Francisco. As you go around the shoreline, you can see the lasting effects of the city's fishing sector as fishing boats gently bobble in the bay and skilled fisherman go about their work. The classic Dungeness crab and shrimp boats, which bring in their daily fresh catches, are still visible.

Gastronomic Delicacies

As you stroll through Fisherman's Wharf, get ready for a variety of gastronomic delicacies to tempt your taste buds. Enjoy delicious seafood that has just been caught, such as crab and shrimp cocktails and clam soup served in sourdough bread bowls. The many seafood eateries around the wharf serve up a wide range of mouthwatering delicacies that highlight the flavors of the ocean.

Pier 39

Is a lively waterfront complex with stores, eateries, and entertainment that is one of the attractions of Fisherman's Wharf. Explore the bustling market to get one-of-a-kind keepsakes to remember your trip. Local craftsmen sell their wares here. Visit the well-known sea lions who have made Pier 39's docks their home and entertain guests with their lively antics.

Historic Landmarks

Fisherman's Wharf is home to a number of historical sites that provide a window into the region's colorful past. Visit the Maritime National Historical Park to view historic ships and discover the maritime heritage of

San Francisco. The Musée Mécanique is a unique museum with retro arcade games and mechanical marvels that will take you back in time. Don't miss it.

Ghirardelli Square

Is a former chocolate factory that has been turned into a bustling shopping and dining area. It is conveniently located near Fisherman's Wharf. At the Ghirardelli Ice Cream and Chocolate Shop, indulge in exquisite chocolate delicacies, or browse the boutique stores for one-of-a-kind items. The Golden Gate Bridge and the bay are both visible from the square in all directions.

Aquatic Park

Is a scenic waterfront park that provides a break from the busy city and is close to Fisherman's Wharf. Swim in the protected Aquatic Park Cove, which offers breathtaking views of the bay and Alcatraz Island. In addition, the park has a beach, picnic places on grass, and a promenade ideal for leisurely strolls.

Entertainment and Attractions

Fisherman's Wharf is buzzing with attractions and entertainment options for tourists of all ages. Take in the great street performers, musicians, and magicians who will enhance the exciting environment. Visit the fascinating exhibits at the Ripley's Believe It or Not! Museum or have a thrilling ride on the storied San Francisco Carousel.

Activities On The Waterfront

Fisherman's Wharf is the starting point for a variety of thrilling waterfront activities. Explore the harbor, pass by the recognizable Golden Gate Bridge, and even travel to the infamous Alcatraz Island via picturesque boat cruise. Renting bicycles or surreys allows you to cruise along the shoreline while taking in the breathtaking vistas and crisp ocean wind.

Visitors from all over the world are enthralled by Fisherman's Wharf's fascinating combination of history, gastronomic delights, and waterfront beauty.

ALCATRAZ ISLAND

Alcatraz Island, perched like a lone sentinel in the center of San Francisco Bay, has a fascinating past that never ceases to fascinate tourists from near and far. This mysterious island, sometimes known as "The Rock," is well-known for housing some of America's most renowned offenders in its former federal prison. Alcatraz still exists as an example of fortitude, retribution, and the quest for freedom.

Famous Federal Prison

From 1934 to 1963, Alcatraz Island served as the location of a notorious federal maximum-security prison. Due to its remote location and perilous waters, Alcatraz was thought to be escape-proof and was built to house the most dangerous and irredeemable criminals of the period, such as Al Capone and "Machine Gun" Kelly. Discover the stories of the prisoners who resided beneath its towering walls by exploring the cellblocks and entering the small cells.

The Battle of Alcatraz

The Battle of Alcatraz, one of the most infamous events in Alcatraz's history, occurred in 1946. Following an armed takeover by certain prisoners, there was a two-day standoff between prison guards and federal authorities. The dramatic events that took place during this intense war made a lasting impression on the island's history and furthered its status as a stronghold that could not be breached.

Today's Alcatraz Island

After the prison was shut down in 1963, Alcatraz experienced changes. The island is now accessible to the public as a historical landmark and tourism destination and is a part of the Golden Gate National Recreation Area. Visitors can board a ferry from Fisherman's Wharf in San Francisco to explore the island's fascinating history, go on guided tours, and learn about the lives of both convicts and guards.

The Alcatraz Cellhouse

Enter the fabled Alcatraz Cellhouse to explore the prison's hallways and gain an understanding of inmates' daily lives. Visit the mess hall, pass by the various cells, and take a look at the locations where inmates would spend their meager spare time. The audio tour offers a terrifying personal description of life on The Rock and is told by former prisoners and correctional personnel.

Escape Attempts and Legends

Despite numerous attempts, Alcatraz developed a reputation as a jail that was almost impossible to escape from. The most well-known jail break attempt took place in 1962 when three inmates vanished throughout the night and left behind improvised dummies in their cells. Numerous speculations about what happened to them are still unanswered, adding to the mystery surrounding the island.

Beyond its dreadful prison past, Alcatraz Island is renowned for its breathtaking natural beauty and diversity of species. Enjoy the stunning views of the San Francisco skyline, the island's rocky cliffs, and the local flora for a while. Watch out for seabirds that have deemed the island their home and are now nesting there, such as western gulls and cormorants.

Alcatraz Night Tours

Think about going on an Alcatraz night tour for a more intense and eerie experience. The ambiance is infused with a feeling of mystery and intrigue as night falls on the island. Hear unsettling tales of paranormal encounters and learn more about the spooky lore that has enveloped Alcatraz for years.

Alcatraz Island serves as a chilling reminder of a time when shackling, misery, and tenacity came together. It is a location that informs and intrigues due to its historical significance, as well as its natural beauty and interesting stories. A trip to Alcatraz provides a rare look at the shadowy side of human nature and the never-ending search for freedom.

NAPA VALLEY

The gorgeous scenery, renowned vineyards, and a rich tapestry of aromas that entice the senses make Napa Valley, located in the center of California's wine region, a destination that draws visitors. Napa Valley has made a name for itself as a top tourist destination for wine lovers and aficionados from all over the world because to its undulating hills, luscious vineyards, and beautiful towns.

Vineyards and Wineries

The Napa Valley is home to more than 400 wineries, each of which offers a distinctive experience and the opportunity to taste fine wines. Wine aficionados can take wine tastings, vineyard tours, and even winemaking workshops at everything from grand estates to small, family-run vineyards. Enjoy the region's renowned varietals, like as Cabernet Sauvignon, Chardonnay, and Pinot Noir, while immersing yourself in the science and art of winemaking.

Scenic Beauty

Unquestionably, Napa Valley is picturesquely beautiful. A gorgeous setting with rolling hills covered with grapes, framed by imposing mountains, and sprinkled with charming wineries captures the eye at every turn. The area's climate is similar to that of the Mediterranean, with warm days and cold nights, which promotes the best circumstances for grape cultivation and guarantees breath-taking views all year long.

Foodie Delights

The Napa Valley's food scene is as alluring as its wines. There are numerous outstanding farm-to-table eateries, Michelin-starred restaurants, and quaint cafes in the area. Enjoy tasty cuisine created by professional chefs who take delight in using seasonal, locally sourced ingredients. When you drink a glass of Napa Valley wine with your dinner, you'll find the ideal balance of flavors that takes your dining experience to new heights.

Hot Air Balloon Rides

Fly high over the Napa Valley's vineyards as you take a hot air balloon flight. You'll softly float above the verdant setting while taking in spectacular views of the valley below as the sun begins to appear over the horizon. The solitude and peace of the trip provide a distinctive perspective on the area's grandeur, making it an unforgettable journey.

Lovely Towns

The Napa Valley is filled with lovely towns that radiate friendliness and hospitality. Browse the boutique stores, art galleries, and charming bed & breakfasts on the streets of Napa, Yountville, St. Helena, and Calistoga. Each town offers a starting point for discovering the local charm and cultural legacy of the area and has its own unique character.

Arts and Culture

Beyond its wine and gastronomic attractions, Napa Valley is a paradise for fans of the arts and culture. Visit galleries, public art projects, and performance spaces to learn about the region's thriving arts sector. Visit the Hess Collection to view modern art while sipping their award-winning wines, or check out the di Rosa Center for Contemporary Art to view an excellent collection of contemporary artworks situated amidst lovely surroundings.

Outdoor Recreation

The Napa Valley invites guests to take in the beauty of nature and engage in outdoor pursuits. Explore beautiful trails by foot or bicycle, go through vineyards by car, or paddle a kayak down the Napa River. The natural beauty of the area offers chances for rejuvenation, relaxation, and outdoor interaction.

Spa Getaways and Wellness

The Napa Valley has a wide selection of opulent spa getaways and wellness activities. Enjoy restorative spa services flavored with regional ingredients, relax in natural hot springs, or attend yoga and meditation classes while taking in the peaceful surroundings. Visitors will be able to discover comfort and tranquility during their stay thanks to the area's dedication to wellbeing.

LAKE TAHOE

Located in the stunning Sierra Nevada Mountains, Lake Tahoe is a pristine gem of the outdoors and natural beauty. Visitors looking for comfort in nature's embrace and exhilarating adventures have been drawn to Lake Tahoe by its crystal-clear waters, breathtaking peaks, and year-round recreational activities.

Scenic Beauty

Lake Tahoe has unmatched scenic beauty. Its glistening blue waters are surrounded by majestic mountains, which together create a fascinating scene. The breathtaking views will leave you speechless whether you're wandering along the lake's shores or admiring it from a beautiful lookout.

Outdoor Recreation

Lake Tahoe is a haven for nature lovers. Enjoy a variety of water sports during the summer, including swimming, kayaking, paddle boarding, and jet skiing. Hike through pristine forests, cycle along beautiful routes, or play a round of golf at top-notch facilities. The area becomes a snowy paradise in the winter, luring skiers, snowboarders, and snowshoers to enjoy its powder-covered slopes.

Ski Resorts

Renowned for having outstanding ski resorts, Lake Tahoe draws skiers and snowboarders from near and far. You may discover a variety of terrain that is appropriate for skiers of all ability levels at the more than a dozen ski resorts in the area, including Squaw Valley, Heavenly, and Northstar. Enjoy thrilling cross-country skiing, downhill skiing, or snowboarding while taking in the stunning alpine scenery.

Emerald Bay State Park

A must-see location is Emerald Bay State Park, which is situated on the western shore of Lake Tahoe. The famous Emerald Bay, a lovely inlet ornamented with a tiny island containing the charming Vikingsholm Castle, can be found in the park. Hike the park's paths, enjoy the breathtaking vistas, or take a boat tour around the calm waters of the bay.

Heavenly Village

At the foot of the Heavenly Mountain Resort, there is a dynamic mix of dining, shopping, and entertainment in Heavenly Village.

Enjoy a gastronomic excursion at one of the numerous restaurants, look around boutique stores for one-of-a-kind finds, or take in live entertainment in the outdoor plaza. The village is a hive of activity and a starting point for outdoor pursuits.

Tahoe Rim Trail

The Tahoe Rim Trail is a fantastic experience for ardent hikers and nature lovers. This 165-mile loop trail around Lake Tahoe showcases the area's varied topography and breathtaking views. Explore the area's natural treasures by setting out on a day trek or a backpacking excursion through forests, meadows, and rocky ridges.

Gamble In Stateline

Stateline, a town known for its thriving casinos and entertainment venues, is located on the southeast shore of Lake Tahoe. Catch a live performance, play some blackjack, or enjoy a delicious meal at one of the resort's renowned restaurants. Stateline provides a buzzing environment where you can unwind and take in the exciting nightlife.

Environmental Protection: The area around Lake Tahoe is committed to protecting the environment, making it more than just a playground for outdoor enthusiasts. The lake's crystal-clear waters have been protected, and efforts have been made to keep them that way.

As part of attempts to ensure the long-term wellbeing of this natural gem, the Tahoe Environmental Research Center offers educational opportunities to learn about the ecology of the lake.

Lake Tahoe is a place that appeals to explorers, nature enthusiasts, and people looking for peace in a breathtaking alpine setting because of its entrancing beauty and almost limitless selection of outdoor activities. Lake Tahoe offers an incredible experience that will make you long to return again and again, whether you're exploring the craggy peaks, swimming in the pristine waters, or just taking in the peace and quiet of its surrounds.

CHAPTER 3

COASTAL DELIGHTS IN CENTRAL CALIFORNIA

MONTEREY AND CARMEL

Nestled along the picturesque coastline of Central California, the neighboring towns of Monterey and Carmel beckon visitors with their natural beauty, rich history, and vibrant culture. From the iconic Monterey Bay to the quaint streets of Carmel-by-the-Sea, these coastal gems offer a captivating blend of outdoor adventures, artistic charm, and culinary delights.

Monterey Bay Aquarium

Immerse yourself in the wonders of marine life at the renowned Monterey Bay Aquarium. Explore captivating exhibits featuring sea otters, penguins, sharks, and a stunning kelp forest. Witness the beauty of jellyfish gracefully gliding through the water and learn about the conservation efforts dedicated to protecting the marine ecosystem.

Cannery Row

Stroll along the historic Cannery Row, once bustling with sardine canneries and now transformed into a vibrant waterfront district. Browse through unique shops, dine at waterfront restaurants, and soak in the lively atmosphere. The street's connection to Nobel Prize-winning author John Steinbeck adds a literary charm that harkens back to the area's rich maritime heritage.

Old Fisherman's Wharf

Experience the vibrant energy of Old Fisherman's Wharf in Monterey. Explore the bustling harbor, watch local fishermen unload their daily catch, and indulge in fresh seafood at waterfront restaurants. Embark on a whale-watching excursion or take a leisurely boat cruise to admire the beauty of the bay from a different perspective.

17-Mile Drive

Embark on a scenic journey along the world-famous 17-Mile Drive, which winds through the exclusive neighborhoods of Pebble Beach and Pacific Grove. This coastal drive showcases breathtaking vistas of rugged cliffs, sandy beaches, and iconic landmarks like the Lone Cypress. Be sure to stop at scenic viewpoints, such as Bird Rock and Cypress Point Lookout, to capture the awe-inspiring beauty of the coastline.

Pebble Beach Golf Links

Golf enthusiasts will find paradise at Pebble Beach Golf Links, one of the most renowned golf courses in the world. Experience the challenge of playing on a course that has hosted prestigious tournaments and attracted golfing legends. Even if you're not a golfer, the stunning coastal setting makes it worth a visit to witness the allure of this iconic course.

Point Lobos State Natural Reserve

Just south of Carmel, Point Lobos State Natural Reserve awaits nature lovers and outdoor enthusiasts. This pristine coastal reserve offers scenic hiking trails that meander through cypress groves, rocky headlands, and hidden coves. Discover diverse wildlife, including sea lions, harbor seals, and a variety of bird species, while reveling in the serenity of the natural surroundings.

Carmel Mission

Step back in time at the historic Carmel Mission, also known as Mission San Carlos Borromeo de Carmelo. This beautifully preserved Spanish mission, founded in 1770, showcases stunning architecture and serene gardens. Explore the museum to learn about the mission's rich history and its role in shaping the region.

Quaint Charm of Carmel-by-the-Sea

Wander through the enchanting streets of Carmel-by-the-Sea, a picturesque town known for its artistic heritage and European-inspired architecture. Admire the fairytale-like cottages, browse art galleries showcasing local artists' works, and explore boutique shops filled with unique treasures. Carmel's dog-friendly reputation adds to its charm, welcoming furry friends to join in on the exploration.

Monterey and Carmel combine the allure of coastal beauty, cultural richness, and outdoor adventures, creating an unforgettable destination on California's Central Coast. Whether you're marveling at marine life, exploring historic sites, or simply savoring the coastal ambiance, these charming towns offer a delightful escape

MONTEREY BAY AQUARIUM

The Monterey Bay Aquarium, located on Monterey, California's breathtaking coastline, is a premier attraction that honors the wonders of the ocean. The aquarium provides visitors with an engrossing and immersive experience that promotes a profound appreciation for the beauty and fragility of aquatic life through its breathtaking exhibits, educational activities, and dedication to marine conservation.

A Window into the Ocean

Step into a fascinating world as you enter the Monterey Bay Aquarium, "A Window into the Ocean." Astonishing views of the famous Monterey Bay are provided by the room's large floor-to-ceiling windows, allowing you to observe the dynamic interaction between land and water. Immerse yourself in the underwater world, which will mesmerize you with its colorful fish, graceful sea turtles, and fascinating jellies.

Kelp Forest

Enter the magnificent underwater ecology of the kelp forest, which is bursting with life. Explore a three-story tall exhibit that depicts the complex environment of the California coast. As vibrant fish, sea otters, and leopard sharks make their way through this fascinating marine forest, marvel at the enormous kelp that is softly swaying in the water.

Wide Sea Display

As you enter the Open Sea display, behold the magnificence of the wide ocean. This vast exhibit highlights the beauty of pelagic creatures, such as stately sea turtles, beautiful sharks, and fascinating schools of sardines. Watch as these sea creatures easily float through the transparent water, allowing you to catch a glimpse of their enigmatic home.

Penguin Habitat

Enjoy the lovely penguins' comical antics in their tastefully designed habitat. Watch them enchant guests of all ages with their synchronized swimming, playful dives, and amusing waddles. Learn about the difficulties these cherished animals encounter in the wild and the conservation efforts made to safeguard their vulnerable habitats.

Touch Pools

At the interactive touch pools, use your sense of touch to experience the marvels of the ocean. Learn about the distinctive textures of creatures that live in tidal pools, such as sea stars, anemones, and hermit crabs. Learn about the remarkable adaptations and complex ecosystems that occur among these coastal jewels through the assistance of trained professionals.

Conservation And Research

The Monterey Bay Aquarium is a leader in marine conservation and research in addition to being a site of wonder and adventure. Learn about the continuing initiatives to save threatened and endangered species, advance ethical fishing methods, and address the effects of climate change on our oceans.

Participate in discussions with the enthusiastic employees and volunteers who are committed to maintaining the delicate balance of marine ecosystems.

Programs for Education

The aquarium offers a variety of courses meant to inform and uplift visitors of all ages. Participate in educational talks, engaging exhibits, and practical activities that explore the intriguing field of marine science. Discover the significance of ocean conservation and how each person can contribute to the health of our seas.

Sustainable Dining

Enjoy a delectable lunch at one of the aquarium's environmentally friendly restaurants, where the emphasis is on serving food that is fresh and locally produced. The aquarium's dedication to sustainable methods is supported by your eating experience as you take in the breathtaking Monterey Bay while enjoying a meal.

An example of marine exploration, teaching, and conservation is the Monterey Bay Aquarium. It encourages visitors to have a stronger connection to the ocean and take action to safeguard the delicate ecosystems that reside under the waves through its engaging exhibits and dedication to marine conservation. A trip to the aquarium is a life-changing experience that inspires a passion for protecting the world's priceless oceans.

17-MILE DRIVE

The 17-Mile Drive is a picturesque masterpiece that perfectly depicts the natural beauty and attraction of the California coast, and it is nestled along the breathtaking shoreline of the Monterey Peninsula. Visitors may embark on an incredible adventure through some of the most stunning landscapes in the area as they travel along this iconic highway, which twists its way through upscale communities, imposing coastal cliffs, and picturesque panoramas.

Coastal Panoramas

The breathtaking coastal panoramas that will unfold before your eyes as you travel along the 17-Mile Drive are sure to fascinate you. You go along craggy cliffs while enjoying views of the Pacific Ocean's broad extent. Every turn gives a fresh panoramic view where majestic rock formations, roaring seas, and immaculate beaches depict the unadulterated glory of nature.

The Lone Cypress

A lone tree that clings to a granite outcrop with a view of the ocean, is one of the drive's most recognizable features. This steadfast representation of fortitude has stood the test of time and has come to represent the beauty and tenacity of the California coast. To take a picture of this magnificent sentinel, pause at the approved viewing area.

Bird Rock

Wonder at the sight of Bird Rock, a naturally occurring rock formation that provides a haven for a large number of seabirds. Watch the pelicans, cormorants, and seagulls gracefully fly over the coastal cliffs as you listen to the waves crash against the rocks. The 17-Mile Drive's colourful tapestry is enhanced by the numerous birds, which shows how intertwined land and sea are.

Cypress Point Lookout

Make a pit stop at this viewpoint for the opportunity to take in the beautiful views of the rocky shoreline. You can see the spectacular confluence of land and sea from here, with waves slamming against the craggy cliffs and the wild beauty of the cypress trees in the area. Take a moment to enjoy the tranquility of this amazing vantage point while inhaling the crisp seaside air.

Pebble Beach Golf Links

Golf enthusiasts will enjoy catching a look of Pebble Beach Golf Links, one of the most well-known golf courses in the world. The best golfers in the world have come to play on this historic course, which has hosted countless championships. Admire the immaculately maintained fairways, the seaside location, and the breath-taking ocean views that make it a golfer's dream as you pass by.

Del Monte Forest

Stroll through this enchanted, lush woodland that brings a sense of peace to the 17-Mile Drive. As you go past imposing cypress trees and through tranquil woodlands, take in all the splendor of nature. The forest offers a nice break from the views of the shore and highlights the variety of habitats that can be found on the Monterey Peninsula.

Spanish Bay

Explore the scenic coastline of this peaceful beach, which is renowned for its immaculate sands and the calming sound of breaking waves. Enjoy the tranquility of the ocean's beat while taking a leisurely stroll along the beach and feeling the smooth sand between your toes. This serene sanctuary is the perfect place to take a moment, relax, and take in your surroundings.

The Lodge at Pebble Beach

The Lodge at Pebble Beach is a classy getaway that oozes timeless grandeur. Visit it to cap off your excursion along the 17-Mile Drive. Explore the lovely gardens, take in a lunch at one of the renowned restaurants, or simply take in the spectacular architecture. Your coastal excursion comes to a suitable conclusion at the lodge, which invites you to unwind and take in the beauty of your surroundings.

The 17-Mile Drive provides an enthralling look at the Monterey Peninsula's natural treasures. This magnificent drive will transport you to the breathtaking grandeur of the California coast, complete with historic sites.

BIG SUR

Big Sur is a captivating location that enthralls visitors with its spectacular beauty and untamed environment. It is located along the rocky and breathtaking coastline of Central California.

This well-known section of Highway 1 provides a spectacular drive through imposing cliffs, immaculate beaches, magnificent redwood trees, and panoramic panoramas, offering an experience that is nothing short of extraordinary.

Bixby Creek Bridge

The Bixby Creek Bridge, a magnificent concrete arch bridge that crosses the canyon and provides breathtaking views of the untamed coastline, is one of Big Sur's most recognizable attractions. To appreciate this work of architecture and to photograph the stunning splendor of the bridge against the Pacific Ocean, stop at the approved viewpoint.

McWay Falls is a magnificent waterfall that drops down onto the sandy beach below. Take in its mesmerizing splendor. This undiscovered treasure is found inside Julia Pfeiffer Burns State Park and may be seen from a picturesque overlook along the road. A postcard-perfect sight is created by the waterfall's sheer grandeur and the turquoise waters.

Pfeiffer Big Sur State Park is a paradise of soaring redwoods, verdant meadows, and winding trails. Immerse yourself in its natural delights. Discover the network of hiking routes in the park that take you through historic groves and provide a sense of peace and a chance to get close to nature. Watch out for animals including deer, squirrels, and various bird species.

Point Sur State Historic Park is where you can learn about Big Sur's extensive maritime history and see the recognizable Point Sur Lighthouse. Learn about the lives of the lighthouse keepers who once guarded this isolated outpost by taking a guided tour. From the top of the rocky point, marvel at the expansive coastal views and consider the difficulties they had while taking care of the beacon.

Discover the unspoiled splendor of Andrew Molera State Park, where the Big Sur River and the Pacific Ocean converge. Hike along the beautiful pathways that meander through woodlands, meadows, and coastal cliffs. Reach the pristine beach and take advantage of a picnic, some beachcombing, or just the peace and quiet of this remote coastal haven.

Discover Pfeiffer Beach, a hidden gem distinguished by its unusual purple sand and majestic sea stacks. Visitors are welcome to explore this remote beach's untamed beauty, stroll down the shore, and take in the magical light show created as the sun shines through the rock formations. Stay until the sky becomes the most beautiful colors at sunset.

Discover the untamed beauty of Garrapata State Park, a coastal reserve home to a variety of habitats. Hike the park's paths as you pass through redwood woods, coastal meadows, and rocky cliffs. Take in the expansive ocean vistas while keeping a look out for local animals like sea lions, harbor seals, and migratory birds.

Dining And Accommodations

Big Sur is a feast for the eyes and the palate. Enjoy farm-to-table dining occasions where delectable dishes are created using only the freshest, local ingredients. Big Sur provides a variety of dining alternatives that will entice food connoisseurs, from quaint roadside cafés to sophisticated restaurants with beautiful ocean views. Choose from a range of lovely lodges, cottages, and campers for those seeking an immersive experience that enables you to fully immerse yourself in the natural splendor of this coastal paradise.

Big Sur's unparalleled beauty and untamed landscapes entice adventurers, nature enthusiasts, and people looking for peace.

SANTA BARBARA

Santa Barbara, which is tucked away on California's magnificent central coast, entices travelers with its Mediterranean allure, breathtaking scenery, and dynamic cultural scene. This lovely seaside city, sometimes known as the "American Riviera," offers the ideal fusion of unspoiled nature, Spanish colonial architecture, and a carefree California lifestyle.

Stearns Wharf

The city's most recognizable landmark is a great place to start your journey of Santa Barbara. The Santa Ynez Mountains and the shoreline may both be seen in great detail from this historic pier that juts out into the Pacific Ocean. Take a stroll along the wooden walkways, look through the interesting stores, and indulge in the delicious seafood at the seaside eateries.

State Street

Start your stroll down State Street, which runs through Santa Barbara's central business sector. Chic shops, art galleries, cafes, and restaurants line this busy avenue. Take pleasure in dining on gourmet food, shopping for local products, or simply soaking in the lively atmosphere of this pedestrian-friendly promenade.

Visit the Old Mission Santa Barbara to learn more about its fascinating past and stunning architecture. This Spanish mission, which was established in 1786, is a reminder of the city's colonial past. Explore religious items and works of art that reflect the history of the area inside the ornate church after admiring the stunning façade, strolling past the well-kept grounds, and entering the lavish building.

Santa Barbara Courthouse: Be in awe of the Spanish-Moorish-style building's exquisite architecture, which serves as a reminder of the city's past. For sweeping views of Santa

Barbara and its surroundings, climb the clock tower. Explore the painstakingly designed sunken gardens while learning about the history of the area via the indoor exhibits and displays.

Santa Barbara Zoo

Take pleasure in a trip to this delightful oasis, which is home to a wide variety of animals. Explore exquisitely created environments and come across exotic animals from all over the world. The zoo provides a chance to interact with wildlife in a tranquil and personal setting, with everything from lively primates to majestic big cats.

Experience Santa Barbara's developing wine scene by traveling along the Urban Wine Trail. A variety of wines from nearby wineries and tasting rooms can be sampled along this walk, which circles the city center. Enjoy the renowned chardonnays, pinot noirs, and other varietals produced in the area while immersing yourself in the city's thriving wine scene.

Butterfly Beach

Take a break on the pristine shores of this stretch of shoreline, which is renowned for its peaceful atmosphere and beautiful sunsets. Sit back and unwind on the fine sands, stroll lazily along the shore, or indulge in a picnic while admiring the Pacific Ocean's glistening seas. For those seeking quiet and beauty in nature, this lovely beach offers a tranquil haven.

Visit the Santa Barbara Botanic Garden, a vast sanctuary that displays the local flora and vegetation, to fully immerse yourself in the splendor of nature. Discover the winding paths that take you through a variety of settings, including meandering waterways and oak woodlands. Explore rare plant species, enjoy this calm garden's tranquillity, and take in the vivid displays of wildflowers.

Santa Barbara attracts a wide variety of visitors because it skillfully combines its natural beauty, cultural legacy, and lively environment. Santa Barbara invites you to enjoy the charm and attraction of the American Riviera, whether you're looking to unwind on pristine beaches, explore historical sites, or indulge in gastronomic pleasures.

CHAPTER 4

SOUTHERN CALIFORNIA ADVENTURES

LOS

Visitors can experience a variety of thrilling excursions in Los Angeles, the global center of entertainment. This vast metropolis offers a tapestry of experiences that cater to a variety of interests and hobbies, from historic sites to dynamic districts. Exploring the City of Angels will lead you to the following remarkable experiences:

Hollywood Walk of Fame: Start your journey at the world-famous Walk of Fame, located in the center of Hollywood. Admire the names of great entertainers etched in brass and terrazzo as you stroll around the walkways lined with celebrities. Take a picture with the star of your favorite celebrity and take in the sparkle and beauty that make this area so famous.

Universal Studios Hollywood

Visit Universal Studios Hollywood to delve into the fantastical realm of cinema. Discover exhilarating rides, studio visits that take you behind the scenes, and live performances that bring your favorite movies to life. Meet well-known characters, tour famous movie locations, and take in the thrills of this renowned theme park.

Griffith Observatory

Reach the top of the Griffith Observatory for stunning views of the Hollywood sign and the metropolitan skyline. Examine the exhibits that explore the universe's mysteries, observe the cosmos via impressive telescopes, and watch captivating planetarium presentations that take you on cosmic adventures.

The Getty Center

Is a top-notch art museum set above a hill where you can indulge your artistic senses. Explore galleries brimming with works of art from all cultures and eras. From the museum's terraces and gardens, admire European paintings, sculptures, and decorative arts while taking in breathtaking city views.

Venice Beach

Immerse yourself in the bohemian vibes and energetic boardwalk ambiance of Venice Beach, where there is a thriving beach culture. Enjoy the colorful Ocean Front Walk, catch some street performers, and take in the California sunlight. Observe people, browse the oddball stores, and take in the distinctive vibe that characterizes this renowned coastal district.

The Griffith Park

Explore the expansive grounds of one of the country's biggest urban parks, Griffith Park. Explore beautiful pathways while hiking, have a picnic in a luscious meadow, or go horseback riding. Explore the ruins of the Old Los Angeles Zoo, go to the Los Angeles Zoo and Botanical Gardens, or attend a live play at the famed Greek Theatre.

The Museum of Contemporary Art (MOCA): At the Museum of Contemporary Art (MOCA), immerse yourself in the world of contemporary art. Marvel at provocative exhibitions that highlight cutting-edge and imaginative pieces by prominent artists. MOCA provides a window into the vibrant world of modern art, showcasing everything from abstract paintings to avant-garde installations.

Shopping & Dining

Indulge in a shopping spree along Beverly Hills' Rodeo Drive, where exclusive boutiques and high-end retailers entice fans of fashion. Give your taste buds a gourmet vacation in various areas like Koreatown, Little Tokyo, or Downtown LA's thriving food culture. Los Angeles provides a wide variety of culinary delights, from street food vendors to Michelin-starred establishments.

Los Angeles is a city that hums with imagination, glitz, and limitless opportunity. The City of Angels offers amazing encounters around every corner because to its famous buildings, top-notch entertainment, and diverse cultural activities. So get ready for an amazing journey and let Los Angeles' spirit motivate you to explore, learn, and make lifelong memories.

HOLLYWOOD

Hollywood, California Adventures

Welcome to Hollywood, the heart of the world's entertainment industry, with all its glamor and glamour. For lovers of movies, pop culture, and those aspiring to celebrity, this storied area of Los Angeles provides a multitude of thrills. Experience the attraction of Hollywood with these exhilarating adventures:

Hollywood Boulevard

Start your journey on this famous boulevard, which captures the essence of Tinseltown. Find the stars honoring your favorite performers by strolling down the Walk of Fame. Visit the iconic TCL Chinese Theatre to see famous celebrity handprints and footprints preserved in concrete.

Visit the magic of filmmaking from behind the scenes with a studio tour. Get a behind-the-scenes look at the sets, soundstages, and backlots where blockbuster films and well-liked TV shows are produced by visiting renowned studios like Warner Bros., Paramount Pictures, or Universal Studios. Discover movie sets, see demonstrations of special effects, and even catch a peek of production in progress.

Hollywood Sign

Seeing the famous Hollywood sign up close is a must-do on every trip to Hollywood. To get the ideal shot of this representation of the entertainment business, hike to the vantage points in Griffith Park or Lake Hollywood Park. Views of the city skyline and the surrounding hills are breathtaking from the sign.

Hollywood Bowl

At the storied Hollywood Bowl, take in the beauty of a live performance. World-famous performers, orchestras, and bands perform at this recognizable outdoor amphitheater. The Hollywood Bowl is the ideal location to take in amazing performances beneath the starry night sky, whether it be classical music, rock, jazz, or pop.

Madame Tussauds Hollywoo

Meet your favorite celebs up close and personal at Madame Tussauds Hollywood. Pose for pictures with realistic wax replicas of celebrities, musicians, and cultural luminaries. This interactive museum lets you engage with celebrities, from Hollywood legends to modern-day superstars, and make priceless memories.

Hollywood Museum

Explore the intriguing history of Hollywood there. This museum, which is housed in the historic Max Factor Building, has a sizable collection of memorabilia, costumes, props, and images from well-known movies and TV shows. Take in the glitz of the golden era of cinema as you peruse the displays honoring Hollywood celebrities.

Hollywood Walk of Fame Tours

Learn more about the legends behind the stars by taking a guided tour of the Hollywood Walk of Fame. Aware tour guides will provide fascinating anecdotes and insider information about the famous people recognized on the Walk of Fame as well as Hollywood's lengthy history and development.

Discover the thriving music and nightlife on the well-known Sunset Strip. Legendary clubs, live music venues, and hip restaurants line this section of Sunset Boulevard. Visit the stores, boutiques, and cafes that make up this famous strip, see a concert at the storied Whisky a Go Go or the Roxy Theatre, or just take in the lively ambiance.

Hollywood is more than simply a locality; it's a representation of aspirations, imagination, and the allure of the big screen. Hollywood offers an excursion that honors the rich history and alluring allure of the entertainment industry with its renowned landmarks, engaging attractions, and palpable energy. So take the stage and let Hollywood serve as an inspiration for you to make your own priceless memories.

UNIVERSAL STUDIOS-
HOLLYWOOD

California's Universal Studios Hollywood is a well-known and recognizable entertainment venue. It draws millions of visitors a year and is one of the most well-known amusement parks in the entire globe. It provides a distinctive and immersive experience that blends exhilarating rides, live performances, and behind-the-scenes looks at the world of cinema and television as part of the Universal Studios brand.

A notable landmark in the region, Universal Studios Hollywood is a large 415-acre complex located in the San Fernando Valley. The park is separated into several areas, each of which has a unique lineup of activities.

The renowned Studio Tour, which takes visitors on a guided tram trip across the studio lot, is one of the primary attractions. Visitors can see the actual film sets, soundstages, and backlots that have been used to make innumerable films and television programs during this trip.

Universal Studios Hollywood offers an outstanding selection of rides and attractions for visitors of all ages in addition to the Studio Tour. There are thrilling roller coasters like Revenge of the Mummy and Jurassic habitat: The Ride, which transports riders on an incredible journey through the dinosaur's prehistoric habitat, available for thrill-seekers. Another popular attraction is The Wizarding universe of Harry Potter, which immerses fans of the adored series in the fantastical universe that J.K. Rowling created.

In addition to its coasters, Universal Studios Hollywood features a wide range of entertainment opportunities. The Special Effects Show displays the technical prowess and artistic finesse that go into making cinematic magic, while WaterWorld puts on a stunning live-action show with plenty of stunts and explosions.

Additionally, there are lots of possibilities for character meet-and-greets, giving guests the chance to speak with well-known Universal characters like the Minions, Transformers, and renowned superheroes.

There are a number of VIP experiences available at Universal Studios Hollywood for visitors wishing to improve their trip. These special tours provide participants access to regions that are generally off-limits to regular visitors as well as behind-the-scenes access and accelerated admittance to attractions. This is a great approach to learn more about the filmmaking process and develop a distinctive viewpoint of the entertainment business.

The nearby shopping and entertainment complex Universal CityWalk also enhances the overall experience. It has a wide range of culinary alternatives, including quick eats and full-service restaurants, as well as distinctive retail selections and a lively nightlife. Visitors can savor delectable meals, watch a movie in the cutting-edge theater, or just take in the vibrant ambiance.

For the sake of its visitors, Universal Studios Hollywood is always developing new and thrilling experiences. It routinely debuts brand-new rides and attractions based on well-known films and brands, making sure that every visit provides something intriguing and novel. In addition, the park conducts seasonal activities like Halloween Horror Nights, which turns the area into a spooky fantasy for visitors who dare to enter.

The enchantment of film and television is combined with exhilarating rides and entertainment at Universal Studios Hollywood, a remarkable theme park. It provides an engaging experience for guests of all ages, from the Studio Tour, which offers a peek into Hollywood's backstage, to the thrilling rides and shows, which immerse visitors in their preferred movies and TV shows. Anyone looking for a genuinely unique and enchanted vacation in California must pay a visit to Universal Studios Hollywood.

GRIFFITH OBSERVATORY

In Los Angeles, California, there is a well-known landmark called the Griffith Observatory. This famous observatory offers breath-taking views of the city skyline, the Pacific Ocean, and the surrounding landscapes from its perch atop Mount Hollywood's southern slope in Griffith Park.

Visitors from all around the world come to this intriguing educational facility, which doubles as a public observatory.

The Griffith Observatory originally welcomed visitors in 1935, marking the beginning of its history. It was made possible by Colonel Griffith J. Griffith's gift, a philanthropist and ardent astronomy enthusiast. His goal was to provide a location where people could learn more about astronomy and space science and experience the wonders of the cosmos.

The Art Deco-inspired observatory's unusual architecture adds to its attractiveness. In addition to its scientific relevance, it is an architectural marvel due to its distinctive characteristics, which include a copper dome and an eye-catching outer facade. Early in the new millennium, the structure received major repairs to keep it as a cutting-edge facility for guests to use.

The Griffith Observatory offers a range of exhibitions and activities for visitors to participate in. The Samuel Oschin Planetarium, a state-of-the-art theater that presents immersive shows about the cosmos, is one of the most well-liked attractions. These mesmerizing performances transport viewers on fictitious trips across space where they explore far-off galaxies, stars, and planets.

The observatory's several telescopes, notably the classic Zeiss telescope, which enables visitors to view celestial objects up close, are another feature. Visitors can use the telescopes to gaze at the moon, planets, and other cosmic wonders with the assistance of trained staff and volunteers. Regular public telescope viewing programs offer spectacular stargazing opportunities.

A wide variety of educational exhibits that explore various facets of astronomy and space science are also located at the Griffith Observatory. These exhibitions provide a plethora of information and interactive opportunities, ranging from the examination of the geology of our own planet to displays on the solar system and the evolution of stars. Visitors can discover the equipment used by astronomers, the background of space travel, and the current state of scientific inquiry.

The Griffith Observatory offers more than just education; it also has breathtaking 360-degree views. The Hollywood Sign, the Los Angeles Basin, and the Pacific Ocean can all be seen from its high location. Many tourists travel here to experience mesmerizing sunrises or sunsets so they may photograph the beauty of the urban landscape from this special vantage point.

There are many options for outdoor exploration on the Griffith Park grounds that surround the observatory. Visitors can go on leisurely hikes, have picnics, or just relax and take in the scenery. A tranquil and lush haven in the middle of a busy city, the park is one of the biggest urban parks in the United States.

The Griffith Observatory doesn't typically charge admission, however there can be a fee for special events like planetarium programs. The official website should be checked for the most up-to-date details on concerts, times, and any supplementary services. Parking is available on-site, and the observatory is easily reachable by vehicle or public transportation.

The Griffith Observatory, in conclusion, is a fascinating location that blends breathtaking scenery, scientific inquiry, and educational opportunities. The Griffith Observatory offers a really memorable experience, regardless of whether you are an architecture or space aficionado or just looking for a spot to take in Los Angeles' splendor from above. It serves as an entryway to the glories of astronomy for visitors of all ages and is a tribute to humanity's curiosity for the cosmos.

SAN DIEGO

On California's southern coast, San Diego is a thriving and scenic city renowned for its magnificent beaches, ideal weather, and extensive cultural history. It is the oldest town in California and has a wide variety of activities, making it a well-liked vacation spot for both locals and tourists.

San Diego's breathtaking coastline is one of its best features. The city beckons sunbathers and water lovers with miles of immaculate beaches, including Coronado Beach, La Jolla Cove, and Pacific Beach. San Diego's beaches offer a stunning setting for outdoor leisure and relaxation, whether you wish to swim, surf, kayak, or simply unwind on the sandy shoreline.

San Diego has a wide variety of historical and cultural landmarks in addition to its beaches. With its Victorian-era structures, the historic Gaslamp Quarter is a vibrant district teeming with eateries, bars, stores, and entertainment options. It is a thriving center for fine eating, live music, and nightlife. Visitors can explore an actual aircraft carrier nearby at the well-known USS Midway Museum and learn about its significance in American naval history.

The famed San Diego Zoo in Balboa Park is a must-see site for anyone who love animals. It is well known for its conservation efforts and has a large collection of animals from all around the world. The San Diego Zoo Safari Park, located next to the zoo, provides a special opportunity for visitors to see animals in their natural habitat.

With its verdant gardens, Spanish Colonial Revival architecture, and various museums, Balboa Park is in and of itself a cultural gem.

The San Diego Museum of Art, the Museum of Natural History, the Fleet Science Center, and numerous more institutions are located inside the park. A thriving center of creativity and entertainment, it also regularly holds concerts, art exhibits, and cultural festivals.

The numerous nautical and marine sites in San Diego are a testament to the city's long military history. The Star of India, the oldest operating sailing ship in the world, and other historic ships can be seen at the Maritime Museum of San Diego. The Cabrillo National Monument honors Juan Rodriguez Cabrillo's arrival on the American West Coast in 1542, making him the first European explorer to do so.

The diversified culinary scene in San Diego will thrill foodies. The city is well-known for its artisan beer, Mexican food, and fresh seafood. There are many wonderful dining options in the Little Italy and Old Town neighborhoods, including fancy restaurants, informal eateries, and food markets. The city also holds a lot of food events all year long to display its vibrant flavors and culinary talent.

At Petco Park, a modern ballpark in the heart of San Diego, sports fans may support the city's Major League Baseball franchise, the San Diego Padres. The park offers a buzzing environment and magnificent city skyline views. The San Diego Loyal, a professional soccer team playing in the United Soccer League, is also based in the city and is available to soccer fans.

The closeness of San Diego to the Mexican border gives the city a distinctive cultural flavor. Explore the flourishing Barrio Logan neighborhood, which is renowned for its thriving art scene and genuine Mexican food. Tijuana, Mexico, a close border town, is a chance for a day trip to encounter a distinctive culture and delight in delectable street food, shopping, and entertainment.

In summary, San Diego is an alluring city that provides the ideal balance of scenic natural beauty, cultural landmarks, and outdoor adventures. With its breathtaking beaches, top-notch museums, varied food, and pleasant temperature, it offers visitors a lively and inviting atmosphere. San Diego offers something for everyone, whether you're looking for recreation, exploration, or a taste of Southern California's distinctive charm.

BALBOA PARK

Balboa Park is a gorgeous 1,200-acre urban oasis that may be found in San Diego, California. It is frequently referred to as San Diego's "Crown Jewel" and is one of the biggest urban parks in the country. In addition to being a lovely green space, Balboa Park serves as a cultural center and is the location of various museums, gardens, theaters, and recreational facilities.

Early 1860s local officials set aside the area for public use, beginning the park's history. Vasco Nez de Balboa, a Spanish adventurer who was the first European to discover the Pacific Ocean, is honored by the park's name. Millions of people visit Balboa Park every year today to take in its magnificent architecture, verdant gardens, and top-notch attractions.

The impressive array of museums in Balboa Park is one of its most distinctive features.

There are 17 museums in the park, each of which presents an own viewpoint on art, science, history, and culture. The Museum of Photographic Arts highlights the beauty and power of photography, while the San Diego Museum of Art is recognized for its sizable collection of American and European art. The Fleet Science Center, which features interactive exhibits and a planetarium, the San Diego Natural History Museum, and the San Diego Museum of Man are more noteworthy establishments.

Many of the structures in Balboa Park are of the Spanish Colonial Revival style, which contributes to their allure and beauty. Panoramic views of the park and the neighborhood are available from the famous California Tower, which is a part of the San Diego Museum of Man. With its lily pond and more than 2,000 plants, the Botanical Building is a favorite location for photographers and those who enjoy the outdoors.

The magnificent architecture of the park provides a distinctive setting for touring the different museums and cultural organizations.

Beautiful gardens can be found in Balboa Park. There are more than a dozen different gardens throughout the park, each with a unique subject and aesthetic. With its calm ponds, ancient Japanese buildings, and well maintained landscapes, the Japanese Friendship Garden provides a tranquil haven. Beautiful ornamental hedges and vibrant seasonal blooms can be found in the Alcazar Garden.

The Inez Grant Parker Memorial Rose Garden enchants visitors with its fragrant and colorful roses, while the Desert Garden displays an astonishing array of succulents and cacti.

The park serves as a center for entertainment and the performing arts. World-class theatrical productions are presented year-round at the Old Globe Theatre, a recreation of Shakespeare's Globe Theatre in London. Every Sunday, free organ concerts are presented in the Spreckels Organ Pavilion, which is home to one of the largest outdoor pipe organs in the world. The park's many outdoor stages and venues regularly host live musical and dancing performances for visitors to enjoy.

There are lots of alternatives for outdoor recreation and activities in Balboa Park. The park is ideal for jogging, walking, or bicycling because it is crisscrossed by lovely routes. Families can also enjoy the many playgrounds, picnic places, and open spaces nearby. The Morley Field Sports Complex has facilities for tennis, disc golf, and other sports, while the Balboa Park Golf Course offers a demanding round of golf in a gorgeous environment.

Balboa Park holds numerous events and festivals all through the year. A beloved tradition, December Nights is an annual celebration with live music, food vendors, and holiday accents. The Park After Dark summer concert series features free outdoor performances by local musicians. Additionally, the park conducts educational activities for visitors of all ages, cultural events, and art exhibitions.

Balboa Park is a genuine jewel in the center of San Diego, to sum up. It gives visitors a variety of experiences with its spectacular architecture, lovely gardens, top-notch museums, and dynamic cultural programs. Whether you have an interest in history, wildlife, or the arts.

USS MIDWAY MUSEUM

The legendary aircraft carrier, USS Midway, is on display at the USS Midway Museum in San Diego, California, a mesmerizing maritime attraction. This floating museum, which is docked in the heart of San Diego, gives visitors a hands-on opportunity to learn about the rich heritage and relevance of the US Navy.

The USS Midway has a distinguished history on its own. It was put into service in 1945 and held the title of biggest ship for a decade. The USS Midway was instrumental in protecting freedom and displaying American military might around the world during its active service, which lasted from the conclusion of World War II until the Persian Gulf War.

Visitors are welcomed with a sizable collection of airplanes that previously took off from the decks of the USS Midway as soon as they enter the museum. These aircraft, which range from classic propeller aircraft to cutting-edge jet fighters, show how naval aviation has developed over time.

Visitors may get near to the aircraft and even step inside some of them, experiencing the cockpit firsthand and understanding what it must have been like for the pilots who flew these amazing machines.

The self-guided audio tour provides an in-depth examination of the ship's several decks and compartments and is narrated by former sailors who served aboard the USS Midway. The expansive flight deck, the hangar deck, and the living quarters, mess halls, and engine rooms may all be toured by guests.

Along the route, engaging displays, videos, and exhibits offer a glimpse into the day-to-day activities of the sailors who sailed the ship and lived on board.

The bridge, where guests can assume the role of the commanding officer and get a sense of the responsibilities and difficulties experienced by naval commanders, is one of the attractions of the USS Midway Museum. Visitors can awe at the expansive views of San Diego Bay, the city skyline, and the nearby naval warships from the bridge.

Additionally, the museum has special displays that focus on particular facets of naval history and aircraft carrier operations. These displays include subjects like the development of naval aviation, the importance of aircraft carriers in the Vietnam War, and the technological advancements that have influenced naval warfare. The fascinating exhibits, historical artifacts, and multimedia presentations provide visitors a fuller comprehension of the ship's objectives and the USS Midway's importance in naval history.

The USS Midway Museum provides a variety of programs and activities in addition to the immersive exhibits. To experience what it's like to pilot a fighter jet or practice landing an aircraft on an aircraft carrier deck, visitors can take part in flight simulators. Additionally, the museum conducts gatherings for veterans, rites of remembrance, and educational activities for students of all ages.

The bravery, commitment, and sacrifice of the men and women who served in the US Navy are commemorated by the USS Midway Museum. Visitors can get a fascinating and instructive peek at living at sea as well as the crucial part aircraft carriers played in military operations. Future generations will be able to understand the significant contributions made by the sailors who served on this illustrious ship thanks to the museum's commitment to preserving naval history and celebrating the legacy of the USS Midway.

In conclusion, history buffs, fans of the military, and everyone interested in American naval history should visit the USS Midway Museum in San Diego. The museum pays honor to the men and women who served on the USS Midway with its sizable collection of aircraft, immersive exhibitions, and the chance to tour the actual aircraft carrier.

CORONADO ISLAND

Just across the San Diego Bay from the city center of San Diego, California, is a lovely jewel called Coronado Island. It has clean beaches, quaint homes, and a fascinating history. This charming island, often known as the "Crown City," is well known for its splendor, grace, and lovely coastline environment.

Coronado Island's breathtaking beaches are one of its key attractions. Along the western shore of the island is Coronado Beach, which is routinely named one of the best beaches in the country. It is a well-liked location for picnicking, swimming, beach volleyball, and sunbathing due to its golden beaches, calm surf, and expansive views of the Pacific Ocean.

The historic Hotel del Coronado, an opulent hotel from the Victorian era that adds to the area's elegance and appeal, is the beach's most recognizable feature.

The Hotel del Coronado is a work of art in terms of architecture and is a destination unto itself. The hotel, which was built in 1888, has a long history and has housed many notable people over the years, including dignitaries and even kings. It is a well-known landmark due to its striking red-roofed turrets and coastal setting.

Visitors can enjoy a leisurely stroll through the hotel's grounds, a delicious meal at one of its elegant restaurants, or just a cool beverage while taking in the expansive ocean views.

The "Village," Coronado Island's quaint downtown district, has a great assortment of stores, boutiques, art galleries, and eateries. The architecture is a reflection of the island's rich history and Spanish influence, and the streets are lined with palm trees.

Visitors can browse the boutiques for one-of-a-kind bargains, eat local food at the quaint cafés and restaurants, or simply take in the lively ambiance and laid-back charm of the island.

The Coronado Museum of History and Art offers a look into the island's past for history buffs. The museum features displays about the city's early Native American settlers, its inception, and the creation of Coronado's prominent landmarks. The tour offers a chance to discover the rich history of the island and the major impact it had on the area.

Beyond its beaches, Coronado Island is stunning for nature enthusiasts. On the eastern side of the island, the Coronado Ferry Landing provides breathtaking views of the San Diego cityscape and acts as a starting point for waterfront dining, shopping, and entertainment. Visitors can hire kayaks or bicycles, take a leisurely stroll along the promenade, or just sit back and enjoy the passing boats.

The island is connected to downtown San Diego by the spectacular Coronado Bay Bridge. It is a recognized symbol of the region due to its majestic curves and imposing stature. In order to see the amazing views of the harbor, the city, and the surrounding area, visitors can either drive across the bridge or take a leisurely stroll along the designated pedestrian trail.

Throughout the year, Coronado Island also hosts a number of other occasions and festivities. At the springtime Coronado Flower Show, beautiful floral arrangements and outdoor displays are on display. Both fans and onlookers go to the Coronado Speed Festival, a vintage vehicle racing event. The island hosts a stunning fireworks show over the bay as part of its Fourth of July celebration, bringing large crowds from near and far.

Coronado Island offers a pleasant getaway, whether you're looking for a tranquil beach vacation, a taste of small-town charm, or a look into the past. It draws tourists in with its distinctive fusion of serenity and elegance thanks to its clean beaches, historical sites, and scenic beauty. Coronado Island genuinely lives up to its reputation as a compelling location, giving visitors an unforgettable experience.

CHAPTER 5

DISCOVERING CALIFORNIA'S NATIONAL PARKS

YOSEMITE NATIONAL PARK

A unique natural wonder and example of the breathtaking grandeur of nature, Yosemite National Park is situated in the Sierra Nevada mountains of California. This famous national park, which covers an area of over 750,000 acres, is known for its majestic waterfalls, sequoia forests that date back thousands of years, and different ecosystems.

Yosemite National Park's stunning granite landmarks are among its most well-known features. Rock climbers from all over the world are drawn to the park's huge monolith El Capitan, which serves as evidence of its geological wonders. With its recognizable shape, the landmark Half Dome presents hikers who attempt the grueling ascent to its summit with an exhilarating challenge. This spectacular and stunning scenery is made up of granite formations that nature has fashioned over millions of years, leaving us in amazement and wonder.

The waterfalls in Yosemite are yet another popular destination. Yosemite Falls, which tumbles to the ground in three beautiful tiers, and Bridalveil Fall, with its delicate veil-like appearance, are two of the highest waterfalls in North America, and they both can be found in the park. These waterfalls' overwhelming strength and beauty, especially in the spring and early summer when snowmelt is at its height, produce a fascinating spectacle that astounds tourists.

Additionally, Yosemite National Park is home to a staggering variety of ecosystems and species. Numerous plant and animal species can be found in the park due to the variety of ecosystems there. Mariposa Grove and Tuolumne Grove are home to some of the biggest and oldest living things on Earth, the huge sequoia trees. With their enormous trunks and imposing presence, these towering giants foster a sense of respect and serenity.

Yosemite provides endless options for exploration and adventure for those who enjoy the great outdoors. Over 800 kilometers of hiking paths, from little strolls to strenuous multi-day hikes, may be found in the park. Popular treks include the Panorama Trail, which provides breathtaking views of Yosemite Valley, and the Mist Trail, which leads tourists to the base of Vernal and Nevada Falls.

For those looking to fully experience the beauty of the park's natural surroundings, there are a variety of activities accessible, including camping, rock climbing, fishing, and horseback riding.

The park's hub, Yosemite Valley, is a must-visit location. It provides stunning views around every corner as it is encircled by high granite cliffs and green meadows. One of the park's most well-known vistas, Tunnel picture, offers a legendary panoramic picture of Yosemite Valley, including El Capitan, Bridalveil Fall, and Half Dome.

The storied Ahwahnee Hotel, a stately lodge that oozes old-world beauty and provides a sumptuous getaway for travelers, is also located in the valley.

The purpose of Yosemite National Park has always been centered on preservation and conservation. Famous naturalists John Muir and Ansel Adams, who worked to conserve and maintain this pristine wilderness, are integral to the park's rich history. Through educational programs, ranger-led activities, and projects centered on sustainability and environmental stewardship, the park still motivates visitors to value and safeguard its natural beauty.

To sum up, Yosemite National Park is a crown jewel of unsurpassed natural beauty and an iconic location that instills awe in everyone who travel there. It provides a special chance to get back in touch with nature and enjoy the grandeur of the great outdoors with its towering cliffs, majestic waterfalls, old sequoia groves, and different ecosystems.

Yosemite National Park is a true gem that never ceases to amaze and inspire, whether you're looking for adventure, peace, or simply a spot to take in the natural beauties of the world.

HALF DOME

Half Dome is a striking landmark of both natural beauty and human achievement that rises sharply from the grand landscape of Yosemite National Park in California. Since it presents an exhilarating challenge and breathtaking vistas, this granite dome has attracted tourists and explorers for years with its unusual shape and sheer granite face.

Half Dome dominates Yosemite's skyline from a height of 8,842 feet (2,695 meters), making it a notable landmark. Its distinctive profile, which resembles a huge granite half-dome, is the product of geological processes that took place over millions of years, including glacial action and erosion. Half Dome's vertical face serves as a monument to the strength and beauty of nature, drawing hikers, climbers, and nature lovers from all over the world.

The trek to Half Dome's peak is one of Yosemite's most popular activities. The ascent is a strenuous and taxing walk that lasts about 16 miles (25.7 kilometers) roundtrip. Hikers travel through breathtaking wilderness, passing through luxuriant forests, next to thundering waterfalls, and through difficult terrain.

The famed cable path, where hikers rely on metal cables and wooden boards to ascend the steep granite slope, is the last ascent to the top. The breathtaking panoramic vistas of Yosemite Valley and the surrounding Sierra Nevada mountains are the reward for completing this strenuous ascent.

Not for the faint of heart, the hike to Half Dome requires stamina, preparation, and a permission to access the cable path. The National Park Service has devised a lottery mechanism to distribute permits due to the popularity of the path, assuring public safety and environmental protection. The difficulty of the walk and the restricted number of permits increase its attractiveness and sense of accomplishment for those who attempt it.

Half Dome is an impressive sight to see even if you decide not to hike up to the peak. Yosemite National Park has a number of overlooks that provide breathtaking views of the granite monolith.

An spectacular panoramic view of Half Dome and the surrounding environment is offered from Glacier Point, a well-known overlook, showing its breathtaking size and grandeur. Visitors can admire the sheer vertical wall, the beautiful granite patterns, and the contrast between the dome and the surroundings from a number of vantage points.

Half Dome's appeal is increased by its importance in both culture and history. The dome has long been cherished by the Ahwahneechee Native American tribe as a sacred location, and it has a special position in the customs and myths of the local aboriginal population.

The history of rock climbing has also been significantly influenced by Half Dome. Rock climbing history was changed forever in 1957 when a team led by famous climber Warren Harding successfully made the first ascent of Half Dome's cliff-like northwest face.

Half Dome is a true gem in Yosemite National Park because of its outstanding natural beauty, strenuous walk, and lengthy history. It stands as a tribute to both the majesty and might of nature and the fortitude and spirit of those who attempt to reach its summit. All who are fortunate enough to witness the magnificence of Half Dome are left with a lasting impression, regardless of whether they see it from a distance or up close.

YOSEMITE FALLS

Yosemite Falls, a beautiful natural wonder that enthralls tourists with its majestic grandeur and awe-inspiring force, is hidden within the breathtaking Yosemite National Park in California. Yosemite Falls, one of the tallest waterfalls in North America, is a tribute to the power of nature and a recognizable image of the splendor of the park.

Yosemite Falls, which are divided into the Upper Fall, Middle Cascades, and Lower Fall, plunge a total of 2,425 feet (739 meters) from their tallest point to its base. Peak flow occurs in the spring and early summer, when the snowmelt is at its greatest, and the cascade is fueled by runoff from the nearby mountains and melting snow.

The Upper Fall plunges down 1,430 feet (436 meters) from the cliff's edge to a sizable rocky ledge with a loud surge of water. With water flowing elegantly down a series of lesser drops and creating a gorgeous image, the Middle Cascades add to the sight. The breathtaking descent is finally completed by the Lower Fall, which plunges an amazing 320 feet (98 meters) and produces a pool at its base where mist rises and creates a cool and enchanting ambiance.

Yosemite Falls' magnificent surrounds further enhance its splendor in addition to its amazing height. The Yosemite Valley, a region of incredible natural beauty where granite cliffs, lush woods, and vivid meadows combine harmoniously, serves as the backdrop to the falls. Yosemite Falls is an absolutely magnificent sight because to its forceful waterfall, thick vegetation, and high granite cliffs.

A pleasure for the senses is seeing Yosemite Falls. A remarkable and immersive experience is made possible by the roaring sound of the water crashing into the depths, the cold mist that blankets the air, and the sight of the cascading water against the backdrop of the park's natural treasures. Yosemite Valley has a number of viewpoints from which visitors can view the falls, each providing a distinct angle from which to shoot their magnificence.

A common excursion is to climb to the base of Yosemite Falls for people who want a closer interaction with the falls. The force and magnificence of the falls can be seen up close on the trail that leads to the base. Hikers can experience the mist on their skin and take in the splendor of the falls as they proceed down the trail. Along with the breathtaking vistas, the hike offers an opportunity to get in touch with nature and comprehend the amazing forces at play.

Yosemite Falls is significant in terms of culture and history in addition to its aesthetic beauty. Native Americans from the Ahwahneechee tribe, who originally inhabited the area, have long revered the falls and regarded them as a sacred location. The falls have served as a source of inspiration for writers, artists, and photographers who have tried to portray its beauty and eternal attraction through their works.

Yosemite Falls is a genuine natural wonder that never ceases to awe and inspire tourists from all over the world. Yosemite National Park's focal point due to its majestic height, rumbling cascades, and scenic surroundings. The falls create a lasting effect and serve as a reminder of the amazing force and beauty of the natural world, whether seen from a distance or experienced up close.

JOSHUA TREE NATIONAL PARK

Joshua Tree National Park is a captivating and distinctive location that highlights the breathtaking beauty of the desert ecosystem. It is located in the dry desert region of Southern California. This national park, which covers an area of over 790,000 acres, is well-known for its surreal rock formations, large swaths of Joshua trees, and a great diversity of animals and plants.

The famous Joshua trees, odd-looking plants native to the Mojave Desert, are where the park gets its name. With their twisted branches and sharp leaves, these strange trees produce a weird and almost supernatural ambiance. Joshua trees, which have evolved to survive in the harsh desert environment, stand tall against the huge desert backdrop.

A refuge for outdoor enthusiasts, Joshua Tree National Park provides a wide range of recreational options. There are numerous hiking trails that run through the park, ranging in difficulty from short strolls to strenuous hikes. Both inexperienced and expert hikers enjoy the beautiful rock formations and rich vegetation of Hidden Valley. Visitors can view historic Native American petroglyphs and take in the calm of the desert environment as they travel along the Barker Dam Loop Trail through a desert oasis.

The world-class climbing opportunities at Joshua Tree National Park draw a lot of rock climbers. With its unusual rock formations and varied routes, the park is a haven for climbers of all levels. The difficult granite and monzogranite rocks that dot the landscape provide enthusiasts a variety of demanding climbing options, from bouldering to classic climbing. Because of its moderate winters, Joshua Tree is a great place to visit all year round for climbers looking for excitement.

Joshua Tree National Park offers a number of scenic routes that highlight the park's spectacular sights for visitors looking for a more leisurely experience. Through the center of the park, the Joshua Tree Scenic Drive, also known as Park Boulevard, offers views of the expansive Joshua tree groves, untamed rock formations, and distinctive desert scenery. The Coachella Valley, the San Andreas Fault, and even the far-off peaks of the San Jacinto and San Gorgonio Mountains may all be seen from prominent vantage points like Keys View.

Joshua Tree National Park becomes a stargazer's heaven when the sun sets. The park's secluded location, low levels of light pollution, and beautiful desert skies make stargazing ideal. Visitors can see a brilliant display of stars, planets, and even the Milky

Way on a clear night. Astronomers, astrophotographers, and astronomy enthusiasts gather at the park's annual Night Sky Festival to appreciate the wonders of space.

Joshua Tree National Park is known for its beautiful scenery and outdoor activities, but it also has a rich cultural and historical past. Ancient Native American rock art sites and old ranches are among the human history artifacts found in the park. Visitors can learn more about the desert environment at the Joshua Tree Visitor Center through its educational exhibits and events that explore the park's natural and cultural heritage.

A land of extremes, Joshua Tree National Park combines a harsh desert environment with delicate and hardy plant life. It is a remarkable gem in the California landscape because of its distinctive geological formations, varied flora and fauna, and chances for outdoor exploration. Joshua Tree National Park offers an amazing experience that celebrates the marvels of the desert and leaves a lasting impact, whether you're looking for adventure, peace, or just a connection with nature.

REDWOOD NATIONAL AND

STATE PARKS

Redwood National and State Parks serve as a witness to the remarkable grandeur and majesty of the old redwood woods. They are tucked away along California's wild and gorgeous northern coast. The towering coast redwood trees that inhabit this stunning protected area, which includes both national and state parks, are some of the oldest and tallest living things on Earth.

Redwood National and State Parks, which cover more than 130,000 acres, offer these majestic giants a haven. The parks are home to groves of enormous coast redwoods, some of which can grow to heights of more than 350 feet (107 meters) and have trunks as large as 24 feet (7.3 meters). As they rise above the forest floor, these old trees, some of which are thought to be over 2,000 years old, inspire respect and awe.

It is humbling to explore Redwood National and State Parks. Visitors are invited to immerse themselves in the peace of nature by the dense forests, which are covered in mist and full of a serene serenity. Through the forest, hiking trails take visitors to secret groves, beautiful waterfalls, and breathtaking vistas.

The Lady Bird Johnson Grove Trail is a well-liked option since it offers a convenient and inspiring trek among imposing redwoods. The Tall Trees Grove Trail provides a more difficult route deep inside the old forest for those looking for a longer hike.

In addition to showcasing the magnificent redwood trees, the parks also contain a variety of ecosystems that are home to a wide range of plant and animal life. Under the towering giants, a lush and dynamic understory is created by fern-covered canyons, bubbling streams, and dense undergrowth.

In addition to a variety of birds, the parks are also home to Roosevelt elk, black bears, mountain lions, and other animals. It is possible to observe how nature is interwoven and to be amazed by the delicate balance of this ancient ecosystem by exploring the parks.

Redwood National and State Parks' seaside setting adds still another level of beauty and charm. Where stunning cliffs, rocky shorelines, and sandy beaches meet the thundering waves of the ocean, the parks continue to the rough Pacific coastline. Visitors can enjoy leisurely strolls along picturesque coastal pathways, see sea-power sites like Fern Canyon, or just stop to admire the stunning vistas of the untamed coastline and vast ocean.

The primary goals of Redwood National and State Parks have always been preservation and conservation. The coast redwoods' populations had been severely depleted by excessive logging, so the parks were created in the 1960s to safeguard the remaining groves of them. These ancient giants are still protected by the parks today, which also make unceasing efforts to protect their habitat and guarantee their continued existence for future generations.

The goal of the parks includes both education and interpretation. The educational exhibits, led hikes, and ranger-led activities offered by the visitor centers within the parks explore the redwoods' environmental and cultural past. The distinctive adaptations of these ancient trees, the initiatives made to preserve and restore their habitat, and the cultural value of the redwood forests to indigenous tribes are all available for visitors to learn about.

The Redwood National and State Parks present an exceptional chance to profoundly reestablish contact with nature. The redwoods' immense size, antiquity, and beauty arouse awe and respect for the extraordinary strength and tenacity of nature. A trip to the Redwood National and State Parks is a transforming experience that leaves a lasting mark on the soul, whether trekking among these towering giants, exploring the breathtaking coastline panoramas, or simply taking a minute to soak up the quiet of the ancient forest.

CHAPTER 6

HIDDEN GEMS AND OFFBEAT ATTRACTIONS

SANTA CRUZ

Santa Cruz, a lively and scenic city on California's central coast, offers a delightful fusion of unspoiled natural beauty, coastal charm, and a relaxed, bohemian attitude. Santa Cruz is a well-liked vacation spot for both locals and tourists because of its breathtaking beaches, legendary boardwalk, and vibrant surf scene.

The stunning coastline of Santa Cruz is one of its features. The area is home to some of California's most beautiful and unspoiled beaches, where golden sands and the Pacific Ocean's glistening waves meet.

The beaches in Santa Cruz offer something for everyone, whether you're looking for a day of sun-kissed leisure, exhilarating surf sessions, or enchanting twilight strolls. Main Beach, which is close to the Santa Cruz.

Beach Boardwalk and has a bustling environment and stunning vistas, is a well-liked destination. At Natural Bridges State Beach, visitors can see striking rock formations and monarch butterflies in their annual migration. A surfer's paradise, Pleasure Point is renowned for its reliable waves and enthusiastic surfing community.

A beloved relic, the Santa Cruz Beach Boardwalk embodies nostalgia and traditional beach pleasure. One of the first amusement parks in California, it has been entertaining guests of all ages since it opened its doors in 1907.

The famous Giant Dipper roller coaster, a carousel, and a number of arcade games are among the exhilarating rides that can be found on the boardwalk. The boardwalk is a hive of fun and enjoyment because to the bustling environment, delectable foods like saltwater taffy and funnel cakes, and frequent live concerts.

The natural splendor of Santa Cruz goes beyond its beaches. There are many options for outdoor excursions because the city is tucked between the verdant Santa Cruz Mountains and the Pacific Ocean. A haven of soaring old-growth redwood trees, the neighboring Henry Cowell Redwoods State Park offers tranquil pathways for hiking, picnicking, and wildlife appreciation. The renowned Roaring Camp Railroads, where guests can enjoy a picturesque train ride through the redwood forest, are also located within the park.

The city's downtown, which is alive and varied, is full of charm and personality. The main street, Pacific Avenue, is studded with distinctive stores, boutiques, art galleries, and warm cafes. Visitors can discover unique souvenirs, learn regional craftsmanship, and become fully immersed in the city's creative energy here. Another well-liked location is the Santa Cruz Wharf, which offers a wide selection of stores, eateries, and spectacular views of the coastline.

Santa Cruz's vibrant arts and entertainment sector is a testament to its free-spirited nature. Many theaters, art galleries, and live music venues can be found in the city, where exceptional performers can display their artistic abilities. Each year, the Santa Cruz Music Festival draws well-known musicians and ardent music fans from all across the area.

The University of California, Santa Cruz, contributes to the lively atmosphere of the city. The campus, which is perched on a hill overlooking the coast, melds seamlessly with its natural surroundings and promotes a forward-thinking and intellectually challenging atmosphere.

Santa Cruz is a mesmerizing location with plenty to offer everyone because it combines nature, culture, and a laid-back beach town attitude. Santa Cruz encourages you to immerse yourself in its warm and inviting atmosphere, guaranteeing an amazing experience on California's magnificent central coast, whether you're seeking outdoor adventures, seaside relaxation, or a bustling arts scene.

PALM SPRINGS

Palm Springs, a desert oasis in Southern California's Coachella Valley, is well known for its year-round sunshine, breathtaking scenery, and unique fusion of natural beauty and mid-century modern architecture. For those looking for a warm and inviting getaway, celebrities, tourists, and outdoor enthusiasts have long favored this dynamic city.

Due in large part to its voluminous sunshine and pleasant environment, Palm Springs is synonymous with leisure and pleasure. The city provides the perfect setting for outdoor activities and rest and relaxation with more than 300 days of sunlight annually. Palm Springs offers a refuge for anyone looking to relax and take in the desert sun, from sitting by the poolside of one of the numerous opulent resorts to playing a round of golf at one of the world-class courses.

The city's spectacular natural beauty is among its most recognizable qualities. Palm Springs has a breathtaking backdrop of craggy peaks and virgin desert vistas because it is surrounded by the magnificent San Jacinto Mountains. A thrilling way to reach the peak, where visitors can take in the expansive views of the valley below and explore the hiking paths that lead to secret oases and breathtaking overlooks, is by taking the Palm Springs Aerial Tramway.

In addition to being well-known for its mid-century modern buildings, Palm Springs is also well-known for them. The Palm Springs Modernism Week draws architectural lovers from all over the world by giving tours of renowned structures and residences created by master builders like Richard Neutra and Albert Frey. Modern design is still influenced and inspired by the city's distinctive architectural aesthetic, which is distinguished by clear lines, wide open spaces, and a seamless fusion of indoor and outdoor living.

Palm Springs has a thriving environment with a range of galleries, museums, and annual events for those who enjoy art and culture. The Palm Springs Art Museum has a sizable collection of modern and contemporary works of art, and the Desert X exhibition features expansive art installations against a backdrop of the desert. The city's cultural festivals, such the Coachella Valley Music and Arts Festival and the Palm Springs International Film Festival, bring tourists from all over the world and add to the city's vibrant and diversified cultural scene.

When it comes to recreational options, outdoor enthusiasts are spoiled for choice in Palm Springs. With its bizarre rock formations and alluring desert vistas, the adjacent Joshua Tree National Park beckons and provides possibilities for hiking, rock climbing, and stargazing. The Indian Canyons offer a peaceful haven and an opportunity to get in touch with nature thanks to their lush palm oases and relaxing hiking trails.

Palm Springs is a sanctuary for dining and shopping as well. The city's Palm Canyon Drive neighborhood is home to a diverse selection of shops, art galleries, and eateries. Palm Springs' eclectic culinary culture, which includes classic steakhouses, innovative restaurants serving farm-to-table fare, and international cuisine, thrills foodies.

Palm Springs offers plenty to offer every visitor, whether they're looking for rest and leisure, outdoor adventure, creative inspiration, or simply a taste of the glitzy lifestyle. In the center of the California desert, its fusion of natural beauty, mid-century contemporary elegance, and cultural dynamism creates an appealing and unforgettable experience.

MENDOCINO

Mendocino is a quaint and attractive town that emits a serene and creative atmosphere. It is located along the wild coastline of Northern California. Mendocino, known for its magnificent natural beauty, alluring coastal vistas, and vibrant arts scene, provides a lovely getaway for those looking for peace and inspiration.

Visitors can enjoy breathtaking views and a sense of being on the edge of the world because to the town's special location built atop rocky cliffs overlooking the Pacific Ocean. Exploration and peaceful reflection are encouraged by the rocky coastline of Mendocino, which is filled with spectacular sea stacks, isolated coves, and immaculate beaches. With its network of trails winding along the cliffs, the Mendocino Headlands State Park provides breathtaking panoramic vistas as well as chances to see playful harbor seals and migrating whales.

The charming architecture of Mendocino contributes to its attractiveness. Many of the town's well-preserved historic structures, which originate from the 1800s, are well-known. Victorian-style houses and adorable saltbox cottages with white picket fences and colorful gardens provide a picture-perfect scene that transports you back in time. Filmmakers have even been drawn to the town's architectural grandeur, as Mendocino has served as the setting for a number of films and television programs.

Mendocino is home to a thriving arts community that draws musicians, writers, and artists from all around. The town is home to a large number of art galleries and studios where tourists may view and buy works created by regional artists who were inspired by the surrounding landscape. Those looking to develop their own creativity can take lessons and participate in workshops at the Mendocino Art Center, which is housed in a historic water tower. A thriving performing arts culture is demonstrated by the town's small-scale theatrical scene, which includes venues like the Mendocino Theatre Company and Gloriana Opera Company.

Mendocino has a thriving food industry that highlights regional and ecological products in addition to its cultural offerings. The town's eateries, bistros, and cafes serve a wide variety of foods, from farm-to-table pleasures and fresh seafood to cosmopolitan specialties. Visitors can indulge in a picnic along the picturesque beach or relish a gourmet lunch while taking in the expansive ocean views.

In the adjacent Mendocino County, outdoor adventurers will discover a wonderland. Majestic redwood trees, beautiful rivers, and a wide variety of fauna can be found there. There are hiking trails, a beautiful waterfall, kayaking, and fishing options at the close-by Russian Gulch State Park. With its colorful displays of flowers and plants, the Mendocino Coast Botanical Gardens offers a tranquil haven where visitors may stroll and take in the beauty of nature.

The numerous annual events and festivals in Mendocino serve as a platform for the town's sense of belonging and connection to nature. Music fans travel from all over the world to attend the Mendocino Music Festival, which features concerts by top musicians in a stunning outdoor setting. The Mendocino Mushroom, Wine, and Beer Festival highlights the region's culinary delights, while the Mendocino Film Festival honors independent films and filmmakers.

Mendocino offers a tranquil and restorative vacation, whether meandering through the town's beautiful alleys, taking in the breathtaking coastal landscape, immersing oneself in the arts, or discovering the natural marvels of the region. Mendocino entices visitors with its unique fusion of unmatched natural beauty, creative inspiration, and small-town charm to feel its entrancing embrace and forge lifelong memories along California's alluring North Coast.

CHAPTER 7

OUTDOOR ACTIVITIES AND ADVENTURES

SURFING AND BEACHES

California's 840 miles of coastline offer plenty of possibilities for surfers of all abilities to catch a wave or just relax in the sun. In this chapter, we explore the thriving surf scene in California and showcase some of the top locations for surfing.

SURFING CULTURE IN CALIFORNIA

California's surfing culture is strongly influenced by the state's historical contributions to the sport, which are embedded in the state's identity. The state of California has a strong surf culture that draws fans from all over the world, from the well-known Mavericks in Northern California to the famous surf sites in Southern California. Learn about famous surfers, delve into the sport's history, and become one with the relaxed way of life that the waves inspire.

SOUTHERN CALIFORNIA BEACHES

Southern California beaches include the following:

Huntington Beach

Sometimes known as "Surf City, USA," offers reliable waves and a bustling scene. Explore the less crowded beaches or join the crowds at the renowned Huntington Beach Pier.

Trestles

Located in San Clemente, Trestles is a premier surfing location renowned for its strong and reliable waves. Professional events are held at this beach, which draws experienced surfers.

Malibu

Malibu is a surfer's haven thanks to its beautiful shoreline and lengthy right-hand point breaks. Explore lesser-known locations around the Malibu coast or take in the famed Surfrider Beach.

CENTRLA CALIFORNIA BEACHES

Central California beaches include the following:

Santa Cruz

Santa Cruz which is a center for the sport of surfing in the region, offers a range of breakers for surfers of all levels. Pleasure Point has a wave that is more forgiving for novices whereas Steamer Lane is known for its strong waves and draws expert surfers.

Pismo Beach

For novices and longboard enthusiasts, this quaint coastal town's laid-back vibe and mild waves make it the perfect destination. Take in the lovely scenery and explore the adjacent sand dunes.

Mavericks

Is one of the world's most renowned locations for large wave surfing, and it is close to Half Moon Bay. Only the most skilled and experienced surfers can overcome this strong and dangerous break.

NORTHERN-CALIFORNIA'S BEACHES

Northern California Beaches offer a variety of beach breaks and reliable waves.

Ocean Beach

Located in San Francisco. It is a location for more skilled surfers due to the frigid waters and strong currents.

Santa Cruz

Although already noted, it's important to remember that Santa Cruz extends into Northern California and provides a variety of breaks along its rough coastline. Discover the region's many getaway options and take in the natural splendor.

Bolinas

Tucked away close to Point Reyes National Seashore, Bolinas provides a more seclusion and tranquil surfing environment. Take advantage of the chance to surf empty waves while taking in the tranquil beach scenery.

Surf Schools and Rentals

Surfing instruction and equipment rentals are widely available in California's beaches, whether you're a beginner or an experienced surfer looking to advance. Your safety and enjoyment in the water may be ensured by knowledgeable instructors who can walk you through the fundamentals. Use these tools to brush up on the fundamentals, improve your skills, and make the most of your time surfing.

CONCLUSION

As diverse as its coastline, California's surfing scene is also. The state's beaches provide countless opportunities, whether you're a seasoned surfer or a beginner trying to catch your first wave. So grab your board, paddle out, experience the adrenaline rush, and enjoy the excitement of surfing in California's stunning waves.

HIKING AND CAMPING

California is a delight for outdoor enthusiasts, offering a vast selection of landscapes and terrains that are great for hiking and camping trips. From towering mountains and ancient forests to magnificent coasts and desert landscapes, the Golden State has it all. In this chapter, we explore the numerous hiking paths and camping locations that await you in California.

HIKING TRAILS

Yosemite National Park

Renowned for its majestic granite cliffs, gushing waterfalls, and unspoiled wilderness, Yosemite provides a wealth of hiking trails for all experience levels. Explore the iconic Half Dome, meander among the ancient huge sequoias of Mariposa Grove, or venture on the picturesque Mist Trail to view the awe-inspiring force of Yosemite Falls.

Joshua Tree National Park

Immerse yourself in the unearthly beauty of Joshua Tree's distinctive desert setting. Hike through the Joshua Tree woodlands, struggle over gigantic rock formations, and marvel at the spectacular vistas from atop Ryan Mountain or Hidden Valley.

Big Sur

Experience the spectacular coastline splendor of Big Sur through its renowned hiking trails. Follow the steep cliffs of the Pacific Coast Highway on the famed McWay Falls Trail or challenge yourself with the tough but rewarding walk to Cone Peak, affording panoramic views of the coastline.

Redwood National and State Parks

Delve into the wonderful world of ancient giants in the redwood woods of Northern California. Wander through the tall trees on the Lady Bird Johnson Grove Trail or explore deeper into the forest on the Tall Trees Grove Trail.

BACKPACKING ADVENTURES

John Muir Trail

Embark on an adventurous adventure along the 211-mile John Muir Trail, traversing the High Sierra from Yosemite Valley to Mount Whitney. Experience the awe-inspiring splendor of alpine lakes, glacier-carved valleys, and panoramic mountain vistas along this renowned backpacking route.

Lost Coast Trail

Escape into the secluded wilderness of the Lost Coast, where rugged cliffs meet the crashing waves of the Pacific Ocean. With its gorgeous beaches, tide pools, and deep woodlands, this strenuous backpacking trail provides a distinctive coastal experience.

Mount Shasta

Climb one of California's most imposing summits, the towering Mount Shasta, a dormant volcano. Hikers are rewarded with breathtaking vistas of the surrounding landscapes and an amazing sense of success for completing the strenuous climb.

CAMPING LOCATIONS INCLUDE

Lake Tahoe

Lake Tahoe where you can set up tent among the lovely coastlines and spectacular Sierra Nevada Mountains. Enjoy a variety of activities, such as hiking, fishing, water sports, and just lounging by the pristine waters.

Big Basin Redwoods State Park

Take in the peace and quiet of California's first state park, where imposing old-growth redwoods provide a tranquil and enchanted ambience. Explore the park's many trails, waterfalls, and wildlife while camping among the giants.

Anza-Borrego Desert State Park

Visit Anza-Borrego, the largest state park in California, to take in the splendor of the desert. Explore the park's distinctive vegetation, fauna, and breathtaking desert landscapes while camping beneath starry sky.

SAFETY ADVICE

Consider elements like trail conditions, weather, and permit requirements when you plan your walks and camping trips in advance.

Carry the necessary hiking equipment, such as adequate layers of clothes, appropriate footwear, and navigational aids.

To have the least possible negative environmental impact and to protect the wilderness areas of California, adhere to the Leave No Trace principles.

Follow safety precautions, such as storing food correctly and staying a safe distance from animals, to avoid confrontations with wildlife.

WILDLIFE AND NATURE WATCHING

California is a haven for nature lovers, with an abundance of species and breathtaking natural scenery. The state offers a broad range of environments that are home to several unique species, from mountain ranges to coastal regions. The best places to see wildlife and experience nature in California are covered in this chapter.

COASTAL WILDLIFE

Monterey Bay

Visit Monterey Bay, one of the best places on earth to observe marine life. Join a whale-watching expedition to see the amazing tricks performed by humpback whales, gray whales, and orcas. Watch out for playful sea otters, dolphins, and a variety of seabirds.

Channel Islands National Park

Visit the archipelago off the coast of Southern California known as the Channel Islands. Seals, sea lions, and bright kelp forests are just a few of the numerous aquatic species that call this national park home. To see vibrant fish, bat rays, and occasionally even the elusive California sea otter, snorkel or scuba dive.

Point Reyes National Seashore

Visit this coastal wonder close to San Francisco to see a diversity of species. During the mating season, be awed by the majestic elephant seals, watch migratory shorebirds along the shore, and see tule elk munching on grass in the meadows.

NATIONAL PARKS AND FORESTS

Yosemite National Park

Is home to a wide variety of animals in addition to its breathtaking vistas. As you wander through the valleys and meadows of the park, keep an eye out for black bears, mule deer, bobcats, and gray foxes. Great gray owls, northern goshawks, and other bird species can be spotted in the treetops.

Travel Through The Historic

Enormous sequoia forests in Sequoia and Kings Canyon National Parks, some of the oldest and largest trees on Earth. While wandering, keep an eye out for golden-mantled ground squirrels, mule deer, mountain lions, and black bears. Pay attention to the pileated woodpecker's drumming and the beautiful singing of the diversified thrush.

Redwood National and State Parks

Enter the enchanted world of the tallest trees in the world, the coastal redwoods. You might come across Roosevelt elk, black-tailed deer, and the elusive marbled murrelet among these old giants. Bald eagles and the colorful plumage of many thrushes can be seen in the sky.

DESERT WILDLIFE

Joshua Tree National Park

Joshua Tree National Park here you may explore the distinctive desert scenery and get up close to a number of desert-dwelling animals. Desert tortoises, coyotes, jackrabbits, and the fast roadrunner should all be observed. Admire the starry sky at night and keep an ear out for great horned owls hooting.

Anza-Borrego Desert State Park

Explore the natural splendors of the desert in Anza-Borrego, the biggest state park in California. Look for colorful lizards and snakes that are lazing in the sun, desert bighorn sheep mounting the steep slopes, and kit foxes darting amid the cacti.

BIRD WATCHING

Salton Sea

Visit the Salton Sea's shoreline, a crucial resting place for migratory birds on the Pacific Flyway. Observe a stunning diversity of waterbirds, including sandhill cranes, pelicans, herons, and egrets.

Elkhorn Slough

Learn about this estuary close to Monterey Bay that is home to numerous bird species. Observe the imperious osprey soar over the river, the graceful great blue heron, and the endangered California least tern.

Observe a variety of seabirds, such as puffins, cormorants, and the recognizable California brown pelican, while exploring the rugged grandeur of the Mendocino Coast.

ADVICE FOR OBSERVING WILDLIFE AND NATURE

Respect wildlife and keep your distance to prevent influencing their routine behavior.

Binoculars, a field guide, and a camera can all be useful tools when observing wildlife.

Visit when wildlife activity is at its peak, in the morning or late in the day.

Always bring drink and sunscreen, dress correctly for the environment and the weather, and wear appropriate footwear.

Join guided tours or employ knowledgeable naturalists who can offer insights and assist with species identification.

The plentiful wildlife and breathtaking natural scenery in California provide countless possibilities for wildlife and nature viewing. The astonishing variety of flora and animals that call California home will enthrall you whether you're taking in the coastline's marine life, visiting national parks, or getting lost in the desert. Experience the Golden State's magnificence and go with priceless memories of your wildlife encounters.

CONCLUSION

As we conclude this California Travel Guide for 2023, we hope that you've discovered the diverse and captivating wonders that the Golden State has to offer. From its iconic cities to its breathtaking natural landscapes, California has something for everyone.

Immerse yourself in the vibrant culture of Los Angeles, explore the historic streets of San Francisco, or indulge in the world-class cuisine of Napa Valley. Discover the magic of Disneyland or soak up the sun on the beautiful beaches of Santa Monica and Malibu. Embark on thrilling outdoor adventures in Yosemite, Joshua Tree, or along the stunning Big Sur coastline.

California's rich history, diverse communities, and stunning natural beauty make it a destination that never fails to enchant visitors. Whether you're a foodie, an adrenaline junkie, a nature enthusiast, or a culture seeker, you'll find endless opportunities to create unforgettable memories in this remarkable state.

Remember to plan your trip in advance, considering the various attractions, accommodations, and transportation options available. Stay informed about any updates or changes, as California is a dynamic and ever-evolving destination.

Whether you're exploring the bustling cities, relaxing on the pristine beaches, or venturing into the wilderness, embrace the spirit of adventure and embrace all that California has to offer.

We hope this guide has provided you with valuable insights, tips, and inspiration to make your journey through California truly remarkable. May your travels be filled with unforgettable experiences, cherished moments, and a deep appreciation for the beauty and diversity of the Golden State.

Safe travels, and may your California adventure be truly extraordinary!

Printed in Great Britain
by Amazon

31164911R00093